For
Aaloka
a wise woman

Sohail
Apr 2014

# LOVE LETTERS
# TO
# HUMANITY

*A SELECTION OF POEMS, STORIES AND ESSAYS*

BY

## DR. KHALID SOHAIL

## SANG-E-MEEL PUBLICATIONS
25, SHAHRAH-E-PAKISTAN (LOWER MALL) LAHORE.

| 891.4393 | Khalid Sohail, Dr. |
| --- | --- |
| | Love Letters To Humanity/ Dr. Khalid Sohail.-Lahore: Sang-e-Meel Publications, 2013. |
| | 239pp. |
| | 1. Literature - Poems - Stories & Essays. |
| | I. Title. |

**Copyright © 2013 by Dr. K. Sohail**

2013
Published by:
**Niaz Ahmad**
Sang-e-Meel Publications,
Lahore.

ISBN-10: 969-35-2621-X
ISBN-13: 978-969-35-2621-9

**Sang-e-Meel Publications**
25 Shahrah-e-Pakistan (Lower Mall), Lahore-54000 PAKISTAN
Phones: 92-423-722-0100 / 92-423-722-8143 Fax: 92-423-724-5101
http://www.sang-e-meel.com e-mail: smp@sang-e-meel.com
PRINTED AT: HAJI HANIF & SONS PRINTERS, LAHORE.

DEDICATED

to

the dream

of

a just and peaceful world

## ACKNOWLEDGEMENTS

Special thanks to

Anne Henderson and Bette Davis

for their creative suggestions

and

Deana Seymore

for her technical support

## CONTENTS

**INTRODUCTION**   9

**POEMS**

| | |
|---|---|
| 1. My Muse | 16 |
| 2. Creative Ideas | 17 |
| 3. Inspirations | 18 |
| 4. A Story Teller | 19 |
| 5. A New Story | 22 |
| 6. Dreamers | 24 |
| 7. Leaving Home | 30 |
| 8. A Social Butterfly | 35 |
| 9. A Darvesh is Born | 38 |
| 10. Now He Radiates Wisdom | 42 |
| 11. Who is He ? | 44 |
| 12. A Human Miracle | 46 |
| 13. Last Night | 48 |
| 14. When We are in Love | 51 |
| 15. Kissing Your Tears | 53 |
| 16. Mystery of Love | 55 |
| 17. Growing in Love | 56 |
| 18. Dream Catcher | 58 |
| 19. Unfinished Novel | 60 |

| | |
|---|---|
| 20. Wind, My Companion | 62 |
| 21. In Search of Peace | 65 |
| 22. In Search of a New Prophet | 66 |
| 23. Waiting | 68 |
| 24. Invisible Chains | 69 |
| 25. My Story | 70 |

## STORIES

| | |
|---|---|
| 26. A Short Distance in a Long Time | 74 |
| 27. Mother Earth is Sad | 78 |
| 28. Roots – Branches – Fruits | 112 |
| 29. A Modern Yousaf's Mother | 139 |
| 30. Bigamy | 147 |
| 31. Open and Closed Doors | 157 |
| 32. Colourful Labels - Empty Cans | 163 |
| 33. Dignified Death Clinic | 168 |
| 34. Island | 174 |
| 35. Devta | 177 |
| 36. Peace Clinics | 179 |

|  |  |  |
|---|---|---|
|  | 37. Sacred | 191 |
|  | 38. Historical Meeting | 194 |
| **TRANSLATIONS** |  |  |
|  | 39. Adult Woman | 202 |
|  | 40. When Should I Expect You back? | 204 |
| **BIOGRAPHY** |  |  |
|  | 41. My Father's Breakdown or Breakthrough? | 210 |
| **ESSAYS** |  |  |
|  | 42. Traditional Majority, Creative Minority | 222 |
|  | 43. Writers and Social Change | 227 |
| **INTERVIEW** |  |  |
|  | 44. Creating a Peaceful World Together | 232 |

## *INTRODUCTION*

Amongst all of my possible identities based on my race or class, gender or religion, profession or culture, the one that is closest to my heart is that of a writer. It is unique to me, reflecting my creative personality and my authentic self. When I am inspired and I pick up my pen, I feel connected to my most honest and intimate self. That is where all my affection and love resides. That is why I call my writings my love letters to humanity. All my life I had a concern reflected in my poem:

**APPREHENSION**

*I am afraid*
*The noise of the outside world*
*Will drown one day*
*The music inside*

I feel fortunate that my inner music is still alive, expressing my creative self. My writings are reflections of my dreams, dreams of inner peace and a just and a peaceful world. I feel so fortunate that life gave me a gift of creativity and I enjoy sharing that gift with humanity.

When I reflect on my life as a writer I can see all the way back to my childhood. I was very fond of story books and loved to read them in my spare time. I was lucky that my father had a small library at home that contained my uncle's poetry books and he regularly borrowed books from the school library. I might have inherited my love for books from my father. I felt proud that my uncle was a poet.

I started writing regularly as a teenager when I was in medical school. I used to entertain my class fellows with my poems and their appreciation inspired me to write more. As time passed I became serious about my writings and developed my identity as a writer. That identity strengthened when I became the editor of the Urdu magazine in the university.

Being a writer always made me feel special. I realized that I had a special gift that others lacked. When I became a short story writer I started challenging the hypocrisy of my social and cultural environment. I wanted to lead an honest life and be in touch with my truth and share it with others through my creative writing, hoping that it would inspire others to get in touch with their truth and not be embarrassed about it. My writings helped me remain honest with myself. It was like my own self-therapy. Maybe that is why I use writing diaries, journals and letters as part of my creative psychotherapy practice.

I find it interesting that of all the languages I learnt as a child — Punjabi, Pushto, English and Urdu — the one that attracted me the most as a medium of my creative expression was Urdu. I used to go to local libraries and borrow books from the sections of poetry, fiction, psychology, religion and philosophy. I must have read hundreds of books as a teenager. Those were the years I was fascinated with

- the poetry of Meer and Ghalib, Faiz and Faraz
- the fiction of Manto and Ismat
- the philosophy of Socrates and Plato
- the politics of Marx and Lenin
- the theology of Maududi and Pervaiz, Iqbal and Azad

and

- the psychology of Freud and Jung.

It was strange that I felt more connected with the dead writers than living people all around me. That was the time I felt I was a member of a Writers' Club, a club that only existed in my mind.

After entering medical school, I got deeply involved in medicine and psychiatry and had less time for my creative writings. But after my graduation from Memorial University of Newfoundland I came back to my creative poems, stories and essays. But I realized that I had changed as a writer.

I had started writing professional essays in English rather than poems in Urdu. Gradually my comfort and confidence in English increased and I started writing poems and stories directly in English. In the last decade I am realizing that there has been another metamorphosis in me as a writer.

When my book *From Islam to Secular Humanism* was published and I was interviewed on radio and television and invited to seminars and conferences, I started writing more and more as a humanist.

After starting my clinic and developing the Green Zone Philosophy, I also started writing as a psychotherapist.

Since I was invited a few years ago to write regularly for "Mindspace" a column on the internet website www.chowk.com, I have written on the subjects of social and political psychology.

In the last few years I have also written many poems and stories in English, alongside translating a few. Some of them have been published in various magazines.

It seems as if the writer in me has been expressing himself as a humanist and a psychotherapist. English is the preferred medium. I want to write in a language and style that someone with a grade ten education can read and understand, rather than at a level to impress readers. I am a great admirer of folklore that is simple and profound and full of wisdom. That is why it is remembered and cherished by the masses rather than just a few academics.

My hope is that my writings will decrease human suffering and increase the quality of life of others. As a therapist I know that when people become aware of the factors that contribute to their suffering they feel more empowered to create a better life for themselves.

I am neither a politician nor a political activist, I am a writer. But I believe that writers can play a significant role in creating social change. They can inspire people to challenge oppressive systems and dream of a better future. They can bring an inner change and prepare people for social and political changes. Writers can play a role in human liberation and give people the courage to be free, emotionally as well as socially, politically as well as culturally. The way other writers' books helped me in liberating myself and getting in touch with my truth, I hope that my books will help others to get in touch with their truth and inspire them to liberate themselves. I want to be a part of human evolution. I receive great pleasure from the idea that those books will stay alive even after my death. It is my humble attempt to serve humanity and I hope my books can continue to serve humanity when I am not around. It is my creative link with my own and future generations. One evening in my diary I wrote:

## WRITING

*The more I write, the more I discover myself,*
*The more I discover myself, the more I share,*
*The more I share, the more I connect with others in a meaningful way,*

*The more I connect with others in a meaningful way,*
   *the more I discover the secrets of making creative friends,*
*The more I discover the secrets of making creative friends,*
   *the more I learn the art of growing together,*
*The more I learn the art of growing together,*
   *the more I feel optimistic that our tomorrows*
      *will be more meaningful and productive than our yesterdays*

In the last year I realized that I have been focusing more on my professional and philosophical writings and less on my creative writings so I decided to prepare a selection of my poems, stories, translations and essays and offer them as an intellectual buffet to my readers sharing different forms of creative expression and a wide range of encounters with my muse.

# POEMS

## MY MUSE

My muse is a mystery. Her visit is magical and mystical. It is always a pleasant surprise. I never know what will be my next source of inspiration. I cannot plan it. I just wait for it. All I know is that if I keep on reading and writing and sharing my creations with my friends, my muse visits me more often. She knows I wait for her special visit. She can appear as

- a beautiful sunset
- a child's innocent smile
- a woman's passionate kiss
- a friend's affectionate hug
- a writer's book
- a patient's crisis
- a sad newspaper article or
- an inspiring movie.

Sometimes she whispers in my silence or appears in my dream. Her every visit is a good reason to celebrate. And I celebrate quite frequently with my creative friends. It is exciting to see my creations inspiring others. That is why I feel fortunate to be a writer.

## CREATIVE IDEAS

*Creative ideas
are like birds
that come to the garden of my mind
sit on the branch of a tree
sing a few songs
and fly away.*

## INSPIRATIONS

*Early in the mornings*
*creative ideas*
*descend on the pages of my heart the way*
*dew drops*
*descend on the petals of flowers.*

## A STORY TELLER

*Dear Friends!*
*Every night*
*when it gets dark*
*and children go to sleep*
*birds hide in their nests*
*and*
*the sun travels to the other world*
*you people come here*
*and sit in a circle*
*in front of the fireplace*
*under a starry sky*
*sipping tea*
*smoking your sacred pipes*
*asking me to tell you a story*
*and I*
*being a storyteller*
*who loves to tell stories*
*share with you*
*stories that I read*
*when I was a young boy*
*stories that were told to me*
*when I traveled to distant lands*
*and*
*stories I heard from my grandmother*

*stories that she had heard from her grandmother*
*stories that have been traveling*
*from one heart to another*
*from one generation to another*
*as sacred wisdom and folktales*
*those are the stories*
*created and shared by our ancestors*
*when there were no books and radios and televisions and internets*
*I have been sharing with you*
*every night*
*stories within stories*
*stories born from the womb of life*
*stories of old and young*
*men and women*
*warriors and hunters*
*kings and slaves*
*gods and goddesses*
*saints and sinners*
*and you listen to them attentively*
*but when the moon hides behind the cloud*
*and the stars look tired*
*and the sacred pipes become cold*
*then we all go to sleep*
*knowing very well that*
*some of you will travel*
*the next day*

*to unknown destinations*
*and some will come back*
*the next night*
*to listen to more stories.*

## A NEW STORY

*Tonight I want to share with you*
*a new story*
*story of a child*
*who never felt at home in his own home*
*story of a boy*
*who was a stranger in his own homeland*
*story of a man*
*who was a step-child of his own mother land*
*so one day*
*like thousands of other men and women*
*from oppressed homes and homelands*
*in the prime of his life*
*in the middle of the night*
*he left his home*
*with his books and clothes*
*and traveled*
*through mountains and valleys*
*oceans and highways*
*to all four corners of earth*
*to find*
*a new homeland*
*where he could create*
*without fear of persecution*
*to discover*

*a new motherland*
*where he could speak his mind*
*without worrying about being hanged*
*where he could love*
*without fear of being stoned to death*
*to embrace*
*a new world*
*where people cherish their*
*differences*
*and celebrate their similarities*
*where*
*he could feel peace with himself*
*and harmony with others.*

## DREAMERS

*He was born in a city*
*where dreamers were*
*either hanged or crucified*
*and years later*
*their statues were erected*
*in the four corners of the city*
*He used to wonder*
*if dreamers knew*
*they would be hanged or crucified*
*why did they share*
*their dreams with others?*
*Whenever he asked this question*
*he was always told*
*in this city*
*not only is dreaming a sin*
*asking questions is prohibited too*
*When he studied*
*the lives of those dreamers*
*he found that*
*some were poets, others philosophers*
*some were scientists, others saints*
*he never met any of them*
*they were all turned into statues*
*As he grew older*

*he wished he could dream too*
*first he felt scared*
*but then*
*the desire became so strong*
*he waited day and night*
*to have a dream*
*Finally one night*
*his wish came true*
*he dreamt that*
*he was a fish*
*swimming in his mother's womb*
*he had water all around him*
*gradually that body of water*
*kept expanding and growing*
*turned into an ocean*
*his mother*
*became Mother Earth*
*and one fish*
*multiplied into hundreds and thousands of fish*
*Those fish*
*lived and swam happily in the ocean*
*but then*
*they saw some islands*
*and dreamt of*
*walking on those islands*
*at that time*
*the vastness of the ocean felt smaller*

*Finally some fish*
*jumped out of the water*
*became turtles*
*and wandered around the islands*
*Gradually those turtles*
*turned into dozens of kinds of animals*
*those islands*
*turned into jungles*
*those animals lived happily in jungles*
*but then*
*they saw trees and mountains*
*and dreamt of flying*
*so that they could sit on*
*tree branches and mountain tops*
*They started to jump*
*their legs became wings*
*they turned into birds*
*and flew everywhere*
*Some birds*
*dreamt of*
*embracing the sun, the moon and the stars*
*they flew higher and higher*
*turned into clouds*
*and wandered around in the skies*
*Finally those clouds*
*started missing Mother Earth*
*felt lonely*

and cried
their tears turned into raindrops
When those clouds
touched mountain tops
they turned into snow
and cold winds transformed them
into snowmen
They started living on mountains
like men and women
had children and families
when they saw their children
shivering in the cold
they descended to the valleys
as rivers
and got divided into tribes
each tribe like each river
had a name and an identity
But those names and identities
made their lives miserable
words
created ethnic and linguistic and religious differences
in spite of being children of the same father
they became enemies
and fought wars for centuries
But then
in every nation and every tribe
some people were born

*who were dreamers*
*some were poets, others philosophers*
*some were scientists, others saints*
*they told their people*
*our stories have*
*similar beginnings*
*and similar endings*
*we started our journey*
*in the ocean*
*and if we keep on flowing*
*in our ethnic, linguistic and religious rivers*
*we will all meet*
*in the ocean of humanity*
*as we evolve*
*we will transform into gods*
*let's dream together*
*as gods are the only beings*
*that can dream*
*But those people*
*did not like what they heard*
*so they*
*either hanged or crucified*
*their poets and philosophers, scientists and saints*
*whose statues now stand*
*in the four corners of the city*
*When the river*
*joined the ocean*

*he saw the hundreds of thousands of fish
he had seen before
that ocean gradually shrank
the fish disappeared
and finally he became a small fish again
and Mother Earth
turned into the womb of his mother
he felt as if God was soon to be born
When he awoke he
felt blessed he had had his dream
but he also knew
if he shared that dream
what would be his fate.*

## LEAVING HOME

*His dream was a secret*
*a secret he did not want to share with anyone*
*but like any other secret*
*it became a thorn in his soul*
*the more he tried to suppress*
*the more he felt perturbed*

*Finally he could not*
*hide his secret anymore*
*he had to share it with someone*
*He went to see his uncle*
*a poet and a philosopher*
*a wise old man*
*who*
*after listening to his dream*
*advised him*
*to leave the town*
*as soon as possible*
*and travel*
*to discover dreamers all over the world*
*and learn how*
*their dreams affect their lives*
*and how those dreams*
*get passed on generation after generation*

*as songs and folk tales*
*His uncle also told him*
*his ancestors*
*who were also dreamers*
*and did not leave town*
*were put in jail*
*or*
*were so tormented*
*they lost their minds*
*After pondering*
*for a few days*
*what his wise uncle had advised*
*he decided to leave*
*Before he parted with his motherland*
*he went to see his mother*
*a tired old woman*
*who had sacrificed all she had*
*for her family*
*and was hoping*
*to grow old in peace*

*His mother told him*
*she was disappointed*
*he did not get married*
*buy a house*
*have children*
*and lead a traditional life*

*He kissed his mother*
*on her forehead*
*knowing full well*
*he might never see her again*
*and left the courtyard*
*When he met with his father*
*his father told him*
*he hoped one day*
*to see his son*
*a religious scholar*
*delivering sermons*
*leading prayers*
*guiding people to heaven*
*He embraced his father*
*kissed his beard*
*knowing very well*
*he might never see him again*
*and left the mosque*

*When he met with his younger sister*
*she told him*
*she suffered being a girl*
*and wished*
*he would protect her*
*and defend her*
*and help her*
*to be free and independent*

*He kissed her on the cheek*
*knowing very well*
*he might never see her again*
*and left the playground*

*When he met his sweetheart*
*she told him*
*she missed him*
*and hoped*
*they could build their future together*

*When he shared his plans*
*and invited her to join him*
*he saw tears in her eyes*
*she said*
*she had to nurse*
*her elderly mother*
*and serve*
*her suffering motherland*
*she could not share his dream*

*When he kissed her*
*on the lips*
*he knew*
*he might never see her again*
*and left her bedroom*

*In the end
When he met with his friends
they told him
they hoped
he would lead them
to fight for
the rights of the oppressed
and the minorities*

*When he shared with them
he was going to leave home
and travel the world
and might never come back
one of them
expressed a desire
to join him on that journey
a journey of unknown destination*

*Finally one dark night
he and his friend
quietly left their homeland
and started their journey
on the road less traveled.*

## A SOCIAL BUTTERFLY

*There was a time I felt free*
*like a bird*
*who could fly wherever he wanted*
*like a fish*
*who could swim anywhere in the ocean*
*like a cool breeze*
*who could kiss any flower in the garden*
*and flowers I kissed for years*
*roses and tulips and bleeding hearts*
*I was a social butterfly*
*I used to go to parties and flirt*
*flirt with*
*young women, old women*
*single women, married women*
*white women, black women*
*I flirted with them all*
*I used to believe in free love*
*And then I met a woman*
*who had*
*smiling eyes*
*and*
*a heart of gold*
*She offered me*
*a gift of love*
*treasure of commitment*

*bounty of intimacy
and I started to dance with her in ecstasy
She showed me
loving one woman in a meaningful way
was better than
flirting with dozens of women
So I fell in love
and grew in love
and enjoyed the gift of intimacy
I learnt to love
the soul more than the body
the essence rather than the surface
When I stopped flirting
and loved one woman compassionately
I had more time
for my art and music
I created more
stories and poems and songs
It was a blissful life
But gradually I lost interest in romance
and was enticed by wisdom
I started to love her
more as a person than a woman
more as a friend than a lover
and that made her
frustrated and angry and resentful
She tried to ignite the spark*

the spark she had killed
Finally she got so disillusioned
she left me one night
And now
after all those
years and decades and centuries
I have become
more contented as an artist
more peaceful as a saint
and lead a celibate life
while she feels free
like a bird
who can fly wherever she wants
like a fish
who can swim anywhere in the ocean
like a cool breeze
who can kiss any flower in the garden
and flowers she has been kissing
roses and tulips and bleeding hearts

She goes to parties and flirts
flirts with
young men, old men
single men, married men
white men, black men
she flirts with them all
She has become a social butterfly.

## A DARVESH IS BORN

*One Saturday morning*
*when he woke up*
*he felt so light*
*he could easily fly like a bird in the air*
*or*
*swim like a fish in the ocean*
*he had been experiencing*
*subtle but profound changes in himself*
*changes so subtle*
*nobody could observe them*
*but so profound*
*he could not ignore them anymore*

*When he got out of bed*
*he felt like*
*a cool breeze of the morning*
*When he looked into the mirror*
*he smiled*
*and spontaneously kissed himself*
*he had never done that ever before*
*That morning*
*he became acutely aware*
*his beard had turned grey*
*making him look wiser*

*he went for a walk*
*and saw flowers in the park*
*rather than plucking them for his sweetheart*
*he let them smile*
*so that they could experience*
*their natural life*
*When he sat near the lake*
*he could*
*feel the cool breeze*
*and hear*
*the sound of the waves*
*He felt in tune with his environment*
*He had never realized*
*rocks and flowers and wind and water could communicate*
*He felt like a child*
*who played for hours*
*with leaves and rocks and sand on the beach*
*While walking on the lakeside*
*he saw*
*the sea-gulls and the geese*
*He went close to them*
*and was surprised*
*they did not fly away*
*He offered them bread*
*and they ate*
*right from his palm*
*When he touched their wings*

*they looked at him*
*with friendly eyes*
*as if asking.*
*Do you want to borrow them?*
*When he looked around*
*he saw a little boy*
*standing quietly*
*watching him feed the birds*
*although*
*there was no exchange of words*
*there was perfect communication*
*between him ,the little boy and the birds*
*they were in harmony with each other*
*After a few minutes*
*when the little boy*
*saw his mother*
*he ran*
*and the birds flew away*
*and he came home*
*That evening*
*rather than reading ten stories*
*he read one story*
*but re-read it many times*
*until*
*he felt in touch*
*with the essence of the story*
*and the soul of the writer*

*That night*
*when he was in bed*
*with his sweetheart*
*he gently kissed her eyes*
*rather than*
*passionately kissing her lips,*
*"Don't you want to make love to me?"*
*she asked in a tremulous voice*
*"No" he said*
*for the first time in his life*
*"Don't you love me anymore?"*
*she had tears in her eyes*
*He kissed her tears affectionately*
*kept quiet*
*and after a few minutes*
*fell asleep in her arms.*

## NOW HE RADIATES WISDOM

He
was born in the house of tradition
was nurtured by fear and guilt
grew up where scriptures ruled the world
felt suffocated in the environment
When he became a young man
he rebelled
and ran away from home
He was so agitated
he could not sit still
He was so restless
he wandered aimlessly for years
in lonely villages
deserted cities
and strange countries
His anger kept him running
running away from himself
And then he met a woman
a woman who
touched his heart
embraced his soul
showered him with affection and love
and washed out
his anger and resentment and bitterness

*He felt free like a bird*
*light like a cloud*
*liberated like a wild rose*
*He found peace within himself*
*and harmony with others*
*And now he lives near a lake*
*in a cottage he calls a lighthouse*
*He goes for long walks in the morning*
*watches sunsets in the evenings*
*He plays with birds and animals*
*enjoys the company of books and friends*
*Rather than following scriptures*
*he follows his own heart*

*People find his company peaceful and inspiring*
*and call him a Darvesh*
*Now he radiates wisdom.*

## WHO IS HE?

*He is like a cloud*
*that quenches the thirst and flies away*
*He is like a cool breeze*
*that fills flowers with fragrance*
*and wanders away*
*He is like a river*
*that passes through villages and cities*
*but nobody knows*
*where it comes from and where it goes*
*He has been appearing unexpectedly*
*and disappearing mysteriously*
*as long as people can remember*
*Some nights he is found sleeping under a tree*
*Some mornings he is discovered feeding the birds*
*Some afternoons he is seen playing with children*
*Some evenings he is lost watching the sunset*
*He is old but handsome and graceful*
*His hair is long and grey*
*His eyes brown and beautiful*
*He walks slowly but confidently*
*He talks less but compassionately*
*He appears to people*
*when they need him the most*
*He believes*

*all precious things in life are free*
*whether sunshine or fresh air*
*spring water or pure love*
*He encourages people to follow their dreams*
*He has no name*
*no place to live*
*no relation to anyone*
*Some call him a father, others brother*
*some friend, others guru*
*Some believe he is a poet, others a mystic*
*He is many things to many people*
*He has been a mystery*
*for generations.*

## A HUMAN MIRACLE

When you meet a woman
from a different
ethnic, religious and cultural background
that you have never met before
and feel as if
you have known her all your life.
When you shake hands with her and talk
and kiss
and embrace
and make love
and feel as if
you have talked and kissed and embraced
and made love to her
hundreds of times before.
When you meet such a woman
and feel as if
two clouds of loneliness,
two fragrances of sensuality,
two waves of passion
and
two melodies of spirituality
have come
mystically and mysteriously together.
When you meet such a woman

*and feel as if
you could be friends and lovers forever
and she feels the same way as you do
you start believing in miracles.*

## LAST NIGHT

*Last night*
*while celebrating Dennis and Maria's twenty-fifth wedding*
*anniversary*
*after a long, long time*
*I danced by myself for hours*
*like that blind and deaf man*
*who kept on dancing after the music had stopped*
*People did not know that he was*
*dancing to his inner music*
*so was I*
*the inner music composed of*
*your thoughts in my mind*
*your images in my heart*
*your memories in my soul*
*It was not just last night*
*rather*
*in the last few weeks*
*once again*
*I feel like*
*going for long walks by the lake*
*reading love poems by myself*
*enjoying looking at sunrises and sunsets*
*listening to birds chirping*
*playing with children*

*talking to the old and wise*
*and*
*listening to the whispers of life*
*I wonder whether*
*I am experiencing*
*love that is radiated through*
*your beautiful eyes*
*your sensuous lips*
*your loving words*
*and*
*your heart of gold*
*I am wondering whether*
*I am absorbing your love from*
*your affectionate phone calls*
*your humorous e-mails*
*Love*
*that is making me smile*
*and laugh*
*and dance*

*Last night*
*while we were celebrating*
*Dennis and Maria's twenty- fifth wedding anniversary*
*I was wondering*
*we had to wait more than twenty years*
*for the right time*
*the right moment*

*the right night*
*to share the secrets of our soul*
*Last night*
*I wished you were there*
*to share*
*your loving touch*
*your charming smile*
*your passionate kisses*

*Last night*
*you were with me in spirit*
*though not in body*
*Last night*
*I could have danced all night long*
*in ecstasy*
*to my inner music*
*inspired by you.*

## WHEN WE ARE IN LOVE

*When we are in love*
*we develop*
*a new sensitivity*
*a new awareness*
*a new consciousness*
*When we are in love*
*we radiate*
*a new spirituality*
*a new creativity*
*a new sensuality*
*When we are in love*
*we start*
*seeing with the third eye*
*touching with the third hand*
*hearing with the third ear*
*the third eye*
*that gives us*
*gifts of foresights*
*and hind-sights*
*and insights*
*the third hand*
*that helps us build*
*new foundations*
*and connections*

*and bridges*
*the third ear*
*that helps us hear*
*the whispers of affection*
*the melodies of compassion*
*the songs of passion*
*When we are in love....*

## KISSING YOUR TEARS

I am so glad
seeds are transforming into flowers
painful feelings into beautiful poems
you are accessing the deeper valleys of yourself
deeper recesses of your soul
I am so thankful
you feel comfortable
to share your dark side with me
If I were close to you
I would have given you an affectionate hug
and kissed your tears
My love,
time has come
to let the emotional pus drain
and let your heart heal
You have a heart of gold
you need a goldsmith to appreciate it
maybe
you were surrounded by blacksmiths
who could not appreciate your worth
and you felt betrayed
Time has come
to heal and grow
and write poems of compassion

*and sing songs of love*
*We are so lucky*
*to be growing together*

## MYSTERY OF LOVE

*My dear sweetheart,*
*My adorable Bette !*
*Our love is*
*deep like an ocean*
*vast like a starry sky*
*soothing like a cool breeze*
*innocent like a child's smile*
*wise like a grand mother's folktales*
*rational like a scientist's discovery*
*beautiful like an artist's creation*
*mysterious like a mystic's silence*
*reassuring like a friend's embrace*
*exciting like a lover's kiss*

*Our love*
*has helped me become*
*a better writer*
*a better lover*
*a better human being*
*I am so lucky to have you in my life*

## GROWING IN LOVE

There was a time
I was ready to fall in love
with any woman
who was beautiful and intelligent and charming
and was ready to fall in love with me
as I used to feel lonely
whenever I was alone
But all those relationships ended
as they were special
but not special enough
to last a lifetime

There was a time
I did not want to fall in love with any woman
as I associated love with jealousy and control
I was afraid I would lose
my freedom and creativity
in a loving relationship

And then
I spent a long time soul-searching
as a celibate person
During that time
I stopped feeling lonely

*Whenever I was alone*
*I realized*
*I did not need the company of a woman*
*to feel happy in my life*
*Gradually I discovered peace within myself.*

*Finally*
*I re-discovered*
*that special woman in the whole wide world*
*that I had known as a friend for more than twenty years*
*who was ready and willing*
*to have a loving relationship with me*
*and grow with me*
*emotionally, intellectually, socially, spiritually, creatively*
*and romantically*
*I feel so fortunate to have such a woman in my life*
*who is growing in love with me*

**HAPPY VALENTINE'S DAY**
*to that special woman*
*who, like me, has discovered the secret, that,*
*growing together is better than growing alone.*

## DREAM CATCHER

When you were a little girl
you used to catch
small innocent dreams
dreams of nice food
beautiful toys
exciting music
and wonderful trips

When you were young
You used to catch
medium sized average dreams
dreams of loving relationships
a nice job and a comfortable home
But those dreams
turned into nightmares
as love got poisoned
with jealousy and betrayal

Now you are older and wiser
and you want to catch big dreams
dreams of creativity and spirituality and serving humanity
as you have gained more knowledge and experience
But to catch big dreams
you have to fly higher

*and to fly higher*
*you have to feel lighter*
*and let go the burden of nightmares*
*To get in touch with a bright future*
*you have to let go the dark past*
*To embrace an optimistic tomorrow*
*you have to let go the pessimistic yesterday*

*To fly in the sky*
*you have to let go the earth*
*Eagles fly higher*
*but they fly alone*
*leaving their families behind*

*You want to catch big dreams*
*they are hoping you are ready for them*
*as they are waiting for you*

## UNFINISHED NOVEL

*Each human being*
*is an unfinished novel*
*that starts at birth*
*and is left unfinished*
*at death.*
*When two human beings*
*get involved in an intimate relationship*
*they start*
*writing a new novel together.*
*When three novels*
*are being written and lived simultaneously*
*plots thicken.*
*Some novels are short, others long*
*Some are artistic, others philosophical*
*Some are boring, others exciting*
*Some are harmonious, others full of conflicts.*
*There are times*
*when we all feel*
*we are incomplete chapters*
*of an unfinished novel*
*the novel*
*that human beings*
*have been writing for centuries*
*each one of us is introduced*

*as a new character*
*but we have to write, act and direct*
*our own roles*
*and get involved*
*in intimate relationships*
*to create suspense.*
*The irony is*
*we can't rehearse our roles*
*Or re-write our scripts.*

## WIND, MY COMPANION

*Wind, my companion,*
*taps on my shoulder, and whispers softly:*
*come along, my lifelong companion*
*pack your bags, prepare yourself*
*it's time to set out again*
*let's climb the mountains together;*
*let's wander through valleys and discover towns;*
*let's explore the next chapter of life.*
*I listened and replied fondly:*
*Oh wind, my friend and companion*
*your invitation sends a shiver down my spine;*
*my dormant pains are brought to the surface again.*
*do you remember, oh merciless wind,*
*the journey of last year?*
*we walked together*
*on the narrow, crowded streets of the East.*
*we explored the highways of the West.*
*together we pegged our tents in shanty towns,*
*spent nights in posh hotels*
*we met people and families;*
*we were welcomed and refused;*
*we did it all in our journey together*
*oh wind, do you recall*
*The children longing for fresh air,*

*left alone in streets, in hovels, and in shabby schools;*
*The elderly so lonely and helpless*
*desolation in their eyes;*
*Young, strong men,*
*marching bravely forward with death riding right behind,*
*Women, degraded and oppressed*
*forced to accept submission in silence;*
*The blacks tortured and tormented*
*in their constant struggle for justice*
*And many families, falling apart from lack of roots*
*running for so many years*
*watching their lives crumble amidst the*
*bounty of their longing prayers*
*Oh wind, my friend,*
*is that what we wanted to see; is that happiness and progress?*
*The wind listened with smiling eyes and said;*
*My friend, you are so innocent, so naive. What a coward!*
*one journey and you go whimpering, dejected and depressed.*
*look at me*
*do you see me surrendering to the realities of life?*
*I have traversed these very roads for centuries.*
*yet, wherever I go,*
*I sing a melody of joy,*
*for you must know that the quitters will be trampled upon*
*while the song lives on.*
*I teach little children to smile;*
*I encourage the oppressed women to fight*

*for their rights.*
*My sweet songs take the elderly*
*to a happy time in their past*
*and their wounded hearts are soothed.*
*I blow my cool breeze*
*to soothe those oppressed behind bars.*
*Wherever I go, I see all, I face all*
*and I try to bring some form of light and hope*
*to my weary friends.*
*There is no place, no person, no situation*
*that will run away from a song of wisdom and peace.*
*I listened to the wind,*
*I heard its message.*
*my strength returned,*
*my wounds began to heal.*
*I did not understand the whole truth*
*but I wanted to learn more.*
*I packed my bags and put on my boots*
*and began to fly again with the wind.*

## IN SEARCH OF PEACE

*There are so many people*
*who are in search of peace*
*Some are searching for inner*
*and some are searching for outer peace*
*Some are searching for spiritual*
*and some are searching for political peace*
*Some are searching for national*
*and some are searching for international peace*
*Not very many realize*
*peace is more than absence of war*
*and it lasts*
*when it is married to justice*
*I sometimes wonder*
*how can*
*angry, bitter and violent people*
*create a peaceful world?*

## IN SEARCH OF A NEW PROPHET

*In the 21st century*
*humanity is in search of a new messiah*
*a new buddha*
*a new devta*
*a new prophet*
*a prophet who has a song of peace in his heart*
*a message of justice in his mind*
*a melody of love in his soul*
*a prophet who*
*unlike the prophets of the 20th century*
*whether capitalists or communists*
*atheist fanatics or religious fundamentalists*
*royal rulers or army dictators*
*would not*
*abuse power*
*fight holy wars*
*embrace violence to create peace*
*and if we cannot find such a prophet*
*then*
*we have to realize as human beings*
*we have reached that stage of human evolution*
*that each one of us can become*
*a messiah, a buddha, a devta, a prophet*
*by*

*getting in touch with our sacred selves*
*finding our inner peace*
*transcending our prejudice and resentment, anger and hate*
*discovering harmony with Mother Nature*
*embracing other human beings*
*rising above the*
*class and ethnic*
*gender and linguistic*
*religious and cultural*
*historical and geographical*
*differences and conflicts*
*offering an olive branch to our enemies*
*our distant cousins*
*realizing that we are all*
*members of the same family*
*the human family*
*the family of the heart.*

## WAITING

*My mind is blank*
    *waiting for a new inspiration*
*My mind is blank*
    *waiting for a new realization*
*My mind is blank*
    *waiting for a new revelation*
*My mind is blank*
    *waiting for a new hindsight*
*My mind is blank*
    *waiting for a new foresight*
*My mind is blank*
    *waiting for a new insight*
*My mind is blank*
    *waiting for my muse*
        *to bring a new gift*
            *a new creation*

## INVISIBLE CHAINS

Whenever we want to do
    something different
    something unique
    something creative
We feel the pressure
    the pressure of invisible chains
    chains of tradition
    warning us
    not to cross a line
    and if we do
    we will have to pay a price
Traditional people
    dare not cross that line
Creative people do
    and pay a price
        to break the invisible chains
        and enter a new world
        a world of dreams
        and unknown destinations

## MY STORY

*My story*
>*is the story of an ordinary child*
>>*who wanted to do extra-ordinary things in life*

*My story*
>*is the story of an ambitious teenager*
>>*who had low socioeconomic status*
>>*but high ideals*

*My story*
>*is the story of a caring adult*
>>*who witnessed human suffering all around him*
>>*but dreamt of becoming a healer*

*My story*
>*is the story of a third world citizen*
>>*who was brought up in ignorance and prejudice*
>>*but wanted to learn knowledge and wisdom*
>>*and raise people's social consciousness*

*My story*
>*is the story of a Muslim*
>>*born in an unjust and violent world*
>>*hoping to become part of creating*
>>*a just and peaceful world as a Humanist*

*My story*
> *is the story of a 20th century man*
>> *living when humanity is at a cross-roads*
>>> *and has to decide sooner rather than later*
>>>> *to evolve or to die*

# STORIES

# A SHORT DISTANCE IN A LONG TIME

There were millions of us, but only a few hundred have survived to tell the story. "Are we lucky to be alive, or are we unlucky because we have to stay behind, grieving the loss of our friends?"

Our mothers laid millions of eggs only a few feet away from the ocean, in various locations all over the world. They hoped that we would be able to travel that short distance to reach our destination; but those few feet took us an eternity to conquer. We were back to our roots, back to the carefully chosen places our mothers had selected to conceal the eggs from human, animal, or birds' threatening view. Only a handful of us have survived to return to the point where the story begins and the cycle starts all over again. We consider ourselves fortunate to be able to reminisce about the past and to have a hopeful expectation for our future.

Our mothers laboured painstakingly in an attempt to protect us. They dug holes in the sand so they could lay their eggs, hoping these eggs would be well hidden from our human neighbours; but they came to the beaches in search of us just the same. Relentlessly the men and women hunted, ravaging the sand until they discovered some of us. They filled their bags and their satchels, and took the eggs away, content that they had pursued and then captured us. If they had taken the time to look back, they would have seen the tears in our mothers' eyes for they knew that some of us would be sold in the market, others would be given to children for the vitamin and protein value, and some would be eaten by men who hoped that it would enhance their sexual prowess; we were unsure whether this was a myth or a reality.

Alongside the human hands there were the birds that employed their sharp pointed beaks to discover us and then break our fragile outer coverings so they could drink our contents before we were even born. We were nothing more than appetizers to them.

Those of us who did hatch had but one goal in mind. We sought refuge in the water; all we had to do was to journey those few feet. But those few feet were full of hurdles, and they seemed too many to overcome. We had no idea which of us would make it and which would fall prey to circumstance.

We were so different from one another and yet collectively, we were members of the same group. Our sizes and forms differed, depending upon the part of the world in which we were conceived. Some of us were as tiny as a silver coin while others were as big as the wheel of a bicycle. Most of us had a helmet for protection; others did not. Under that hardened facade we were soft and tender, a vulnerability we chose not to disclose. When we awoke, and started to crawl towards the water we were an army of great magnitude, at least in number.

The first enemy that we encountered were the predatory birds. They were circling the area, or sitting on rocks, waiting for us to emerge. When we started to move they screamed in excitement and swooped down to attack us. We were helpless because our size was too diminutive and we lacked strength.

The second of our foes were the lizards. They appeared out of nowhere, scooping us up with ravenous mouths. They were enormous in contrast to us, and we were unable to defend ourselves. In one big swoop, they ate us alive.

If we were fortunate enough to survive the first two enemies we were attacked by the third — the crabs. As fierce and dangerous as they appeared, we still fought back hoping that this time we had a chance because, at least, they were equal to us in size. They pulled us farther away from the ocean while we pushed back, hoping to get closer to the water. This dance of death would often go on for hours. Neither of us would give up. For a few minutes one side would succeed and then exhaustion took over and the other side would regain its strength. It would have been easier to succumb yet we were known for our stamina: the folk tale of the tortoise and the hare boasts of our endurance; we are marathon runners, slow but consistent. And so our battle with the crabs went on.

Some of our battles we won, while others we lost. Our only strength was in the size of our army; we were so many in number that a handful of birds, reptiles, or human beings could kill only so many of us.

Finally a few of us were able to come close enough to the water that we could feel and smell the tide; then a predator would attack with its claws. All there was left to do was to hope that our guardian angel would be watching over us. We did the best we could, but still we could not embrace the ocean. Those of us who were blessed with good luck were dropped from the mouths of the predators which placed us a few inches closer to the water's edge.

The most unfortunate of the deaths occurred when some of us were accidentally trampled under the heavy bodies of our mothers who sought refuge in the water as well.

Once we had reached the water we felt reasonably safe until a few of us were grasped by fish; it was then that we realized that we weren't safe even in the ocean, the one abode that we so desperately tried to reach. Those of us who grew and became strong enough to face our enemies and the harsh environment knew that we had to repeat the tradition. We had to follow in the footsteps of our ancestors and go back to the shore to dig our holes and lay our eggs. We had to repeat that comic yet tragic drama, generation after generation. We had to lay at least one hundred eggs for one egg to survive and reach adulthood; the few meagre feet reappeared hauntingly in our minds.

We are optimistic. Perhaps our human neighbours have become friendlier; perhaps they have become enlightened. We only hope that they begin to believe in co-existence, and that they will preserve our eggs so that we can safely hatch. Only then can we identify ourselves with our caring friends who share this earth so that we have only to produce one or two babies and feel confident that they will survive. It is the cynical ones we fear, who remind us that there is a distinction between the privileged and less fortunate; in the Western world the privileged can afford to have one or two children while others in the Third world still have to give birth to dozens of children to ensure that one will survive—survive and travel a short distance from their birth place to school to the workplace. It is but a short distance that is covered over a long period of time, sometimes generations.

## MOTHER EARTH IS SAD

Tonight

when you asked me to read you a bedtime story

I got lost in the labyrinth of my past

I remember

reading you bedtime stories

when you were a little girl

stories

that grandmothers read to their

 granddaughters

stories

in which princes marry princesses and live happily ever after

stories

that are based on fantasy rather than reality

stories

that act as lullabies and put little girls to sleep. But the story I am going to share with you tonight is different from all the stories that I shared with you when you were just a child. It is a new story. It is a story that will take the whole night to tell. You are a young woman now and you can easily miss a night of sleep. This story you will one day share with your own granddaughter and it will be passed on from one generation to the next and cherished by the children of our future generations.

It is a story of a mother and a motherland in which the mother was separated from her children as they decided to leave home and explore other worlds. Those children lived a life of exile and adopted other motherlands. Their natural mother, who had nurtured them with her own blood and fed them with her milk, became lonely and sad and felt very alone in her old age. This is the story of that sad mother.

My Dear Child!
Once a mother or a motherland
becomes so old and barren that
her body becomes a cactus,
her hands start to tremble
her eyesight becomes weak
and
her breasts secrete poison rather than milk and honey
then, when
her children try to embrace her
they get bruised and hurt,
they cry and bleed,
they leave their mother
and go to far off lands
and never return
and even when they do return
for short visits,
they come
out of sympathy
and pity
and a feeling of obligation.
They return
to console her,
and not
out of genuine

**LOVE LETTERS TO HUMANITY**

caring
        and affection
              and love
and that delicate and sensitive thread
that binds them together
is torn apart.

The umbilical cord is severed;
the sacred relationship is wounded.
They lick their wounds,
mother on one side
children on the other.

My Darling!
After I returned from my world trip
in which I visited
my children and grandchildren
who are spread
from North America to South Africa
from Western Europe to the Middle East
where they have made
those foreign lands their homes,
I have been experiencing sleepless nights.
In the last few months
I have consulted numerous
        doctors,
               hakims,
                      medicine men

        and

           spiritual healers

Some say

  my illness is physical,

Others say

  it is psychological,

while some others insist

  it is spiritual.

It is an illness

  that has swept

    my whole body,

      my whole being.

It is an illness

  that has no name

    no treatment

      no remedy

        no solace.

It is an illness

  that haunts

    every vein of my body

    every cell of my mind

    every depth of my soul.

It is an illness

  that has poisoned

    my every hope

    my every desire

    my every prayer.

My Child!

If I were a poetess or a writer I would have artistically and eloquently written my biography and the history of my motherland, but I have neither a pen in my hand nor a university degree in my pocket. I am an illiterate and uneducated person in the eyes of others. I am well aware that it is not because I was stupid; rather, I was smarter and brighter than my brothers, but I was deprived of a formal education because I was a girl. In the environment in which I was raised, girls were not allowed to go to schools, colleges and universities. They were trained to do household work—taught to cook, clean and wash. They were conditioned to sacrifice their lives and their futures for their families. So while my brothers achieved university degrees, I looked after the household duties. I never acquired the wealth of education. I remained poor and one can imagine the future of a community where half of the population is raised in the darkness of ignorance. They cannot read or write a word, they cannot sign legal documents. But I loved knowledge so I started to study the book of life and realized that to learn about life one does not have to study textbooks or have a formal education. I met so many uneducated people who have greater insight into life and are wiser than those who have university degrees.

Dear Child!

I am so glad that you obtained your Masters in Journalism. I am so proud of you for having achieved such a heightened sense of social consciousness that you write the stories of the oppressed and the deprived of our society. Perhaps one day you can write my story, the story of your own grandmother, a story that is not only the story of our family but also of our time.

It is the story of our motherland that we call Punjab, a land that embraces five rivers which irrigate our farms. The farms produce crops for the farmers. Unfortunately the farmers never reap the fruits of what they sew. While those farmers feed the whole country their own children go to bed hungry and they don't have enough money to marry off their daughters.

Darling!
Whether they are rivers of Punjab
or any other motherland
they are all related
to the tall, graceful mountains,
the mountains who wear crowns of snow
upon their heads.
When those crowns
melt in summer
they descend to the valleys
and flow as rivers.
As rivers
they acquire names and identities
but then,
one day those rivers
merge into the ocean.
In that process
who knows
what they gain

and what they lose.

Dear Daughter!

    Our family is not any different from those rivers. We started our journey from the mountains and valleys of Kashmir, where our forefathers and foremothers used to live. Kashmir was always known for

    chirping birds

    fragrant flowers

    starry nights

    sunny days

    and

    beautiful lakes.

People
from all over the world
used to come
to spend summers in Kashmir,
a paradise on Earth.
But then
our ancestors had to leave
that paradise.
They packed their belongings
and carried their tents
on their backs.
They said goodbye
to their motherland.
It was the first immigration
within our family;

it turned out to be
the first of many.
When people
leave their home
they sever their bond
with their homeland
and then they are unable to find peace
in any other homeland.
So
the caravan of our family left Kashmir
and came to Punjab
where they
attached their tents and their hearts
to the new land.
Those folks
      who spoke Kashmiri
      as their mother tongue
      came to speak Punjabi fluently
      two generations later.
They believed
      they had found a new homeland
      but it was an illusion.
The happiness,
      the hope,
      the bond,
      the peace
      they had discovered
      was only temporary.

## LOVE LETTERS TO HUMANITY

The sword of History fell
    and
        cut the hearts into two.

Not only Kashmir and Bengal
    but also
        the motherland of Punjab
            became divided into two,
                and once again
                      we became refugees.

We had to move
from East Punjab to West Punjab.
At first we experienced
the massacre of Jalianwala Bagh
and lost
many of our dear ones
and then
one day
at midnight
one motherland became two
and two brothers
who were born from the same womb
breast-fed by the same mother
spoke the same mother tongue
cultivated the same farms
became bloodthirsty stepbrothers.
They reminded us of the time
when

Habeel and Qabeel
two sons of Adam
fought
and one brother killed the other.

My Sweetheart!
The second immigration
was far more painful than the first.

In the first
our ancestors had only lost their homes
while in the second
daughters lost their innocence
and fathers
their pride.
The disasters of the first
we heard with our ears,
the disgrace of the second
we saw with our eyes.
God knows how many
mornings turned sad,
afternoons remorseful
and
evenings depressed.
I used to snuggle up
with my two daughters and two sons
in bed;
sleepless nights were spent

in fear.
Your grandfather,
who was a Kashmiri shawl merchant
in Calcutta
used to be away from home
for months at a time
and I
used to look after
the home and the children
all by myself.
Those days were hard.
Every news that we received
was bad news.
My sister and brother left for Lahore and wanted me and the children
to join them but I stayed behind and waited for your grandpa.
Every day that passed
seemed like a decade
every night like a century.
Finally
when your grandfather arrived,
we decided to leave.
With empty hands
we moved on.
We left behind
our property,
the business
and a furnished home.

Your grandfather had a good friend who used to look after us when he was away. He loved us and we trusted him. The day we decided to move, your grandfather's friend went to get us a taxi so that we could go to the railway station. He never came back.

We waited impatiently for him for an hour, and then another, until finally three hours or more had passed. When he did not return we realized he had been killed by a sword, a kirpan or a gun.

So your grandfather went out himself to get a taxi. It was a risky affair. Halfway he met a Sardarji, his childhood buddy.

"Khawaja Sahib! Where are you going?" he asked.

"To get a taxi for the children."

"Don't go any further. If you approach the cross roads you will be killed. Go back. I will try my best to get a taxi."

After a few minutes he came with a taxi, hid us in it and took us to the railway station.

When we arrived at the station we found out that the train had been waiting for the past forty-eight hours. The driver was afraid to leave the station as he did not want the train ambushed and the passengers subsequently killed. People were clinging to the train like bees to a honeycomb. People were sitting in the seats, on the floor, and on the steps and hanging from the windows. We asked the children to wait, perhaps for a miracle, for surely a miracle was needed to transport us from the dangers of Amritsar to the safety of Lahore.

After twenty-four hours of waiting, the train whistle blew and we were ready to depart. Your grandpa had a dangerous but novel idea. "Why don't we travel on the roof?" We all climbed over people's shoulders and got to the roof of the train, risking our lives in doing so.

The train left the station and started to crawl cautiously, as if afraid. It was terrifying as we slowly moved towards the border. It took twelve hours to cover a two-hour journey. When we arrived at the Lahore station everybody was relieved to have escaped what seemed a death sentence. Your grandfather and I had tears in our eyes. Mine were tears of joy, happy that my children had been saved; his were tears of sadness, as he had lost his friend. That loss wounded your grandfather's heart. It was a wound that never healed. That immigration was painful and heartbreaking. It was like crossing a river

    a river of blood,

    a river of fire,

    a river of divided loyalties

        broken faiths

        and shattered dreams.

Some stayed behind,

    some drowned halfway

    and some arrived at the other shore.

We will never know for sure what we had lost and what we had gained on that journey.

Those who arrived in the promised land found a dedicated gardener and joined him in sewing fresh seeds.

They prepared and offered

    the soil of hope

        the sunshine of ambitions

            the blood of sacrifice

        and

            the water of prayers.

They hoped that when the plants grew and became strong shady trees, they would enjoy the fruits of peace, justice and friendship.

Before the first year was over the gardener died. He suffered from tuberculosis. He had spent sleepless nights pacing back and forth in his room worrying about the members of his new family in the new motherland. He used to dream about the trees of democracy, secular views and humanitarian values in his garden.

The death of the gardener was a bad omen for the garden.

A stormy wind started to blow.

It was a wind that uprooted the new

>    plants and replaced them with seeds
>
>    of prejudice and religious
>
>    fanaticism.

The wind blew out the candles of

>    tolerance and acceptance.

Friends who seemed honest and caring

>    turned selfish and sadistic.

The golden dream of the new motherland

>    turned into a nightmare.

My sister in Lahore

>    who had a small home
>
>    but a big heart
>
>    let us stay with her.

We faced pain

>    poverty
>
>    prejudice
>
>    but remained patient.

I endured hardships
> but did not complain

I washed clothes
> with chilling cold water in winters
>
> baked bread
>
> on burning coals
>
> in hot summers.

I worked hard
> and was able to send
>
> my four children
>
> to schools, colleges and
>
> universities.

I had promised myself that I would treat my daughters and sons alike and expose them both to higher education. I was proud to fulfil my promise to myself.

When your older uncle passed his Masters examination and stood first in the university, I was ecstatic. I distributed sweets among my friends and relatives and food to the poor. That was the first day in the new homeland when the whole family was euphoric.

Your uncle started to teach in the university and we could then afford a bigger home, a home that had a shady tree in the backyard. I remember how we used to rest in the shade in the summer time. It used to be so hot that the sparrows, the pigeons and the hens would rest under the shade of that tree as well. Your uncle soon established himself in the academic circles. He was a bright and a dedicated teacher. He not only taught his students the information in the textbooks—he also shared his philosophy about peace

        justice

        harmony

        cooperation

        and working together

        for a better future.

He inspired his students

        to be builders

        of a new homeland

        a homeland that

        they could be proud of one day.

But that dream did not last very long.

As time passed,

        the winds of intolerance and prejudice

        became stronger and stronger

        and struck

        a certain segment of the community.

A certain minority

        became the scapegoat.

Their members were declared outsiders.

They were socially boycotted.

They were publicly insulted.

People threw garbage in front of their homes.

They were deprived of their civil rights.

Their patriotism and faith were questioned.

They were forced to defend themselves.

Darling,

Whenever children start to feel as if
>they are stepchildren in their own homes, it is a bad omen
>for the motherland.

Whenever the waves of anger, resentment and
>bitterness run high, the feelings of
>good will are drowned.

Whenever the flames of prejudice and
>intolerance go wild, the bonds of caring
>and cooperation turn into ashes.

People who were hoping to live in the
>promised land found themselves in a
>war zone.

Holy war was declared in the city of peace.

A close friend of your uncle, who was a caring, nurturing and dedicated teacher and had helped his students to learn how to read and write and develop their characters, was caught in the crossfire.

He was declared an atheist and condemned to be stoned.

The students surrounded his home and confiscated his academic and holy books, his wife's clothes and the children's toys. They piled the family's belongings outside the house and set them on fire. Murder would have been committed if the family had been at home that day.

When your uncle tried to stop them, they said, "Go away and be thankful we are not burning your home."

That incident broke your uncle's heart, and when he returned home, he and your grandfather cried the whole night together. They wept and tried to console each other. Your grandfather said that he had lost a friend and hoped to gain a motherland where people would be able to transcend their anger and bitterness. He hoped for a land where people could live in peace and harmony. He was shocked to see people declaring holy war against their own brethren. That reminded him of Jung-e-Jamel, in which Mohammed's wife Aisha and cousin Caliph Ali were on opposite sides. It was hard for people to decide who was in the right and who was in the wrong.

Your uncle was so troubled by his friend's predicament that he wore black clothes for weeks. He decided that a motherland in which students do not respect their teachers was not worthwhile. To protect his self-respect he left home one night and never returned. He was the first son to leave his mother, his motherland, and emigrate to unknown destinations. He did not look back. He did not want to see tears in his mother's eyes. He knew those tears would make it difficult for him to part.

For a long time I went looking for him. I wandered the streets. I went to numerous schools and friends' houses searching for him. I felt as if he was like Prophet Yousaf who was thrown into a well by his stepbrothers. I wept like Yousaf's father, the prophet Jacob, but it was all in vain.

Finally I got a letter in the mail. Your uncle and his friend whose home had been burnt by the students had left the country. Your uncle's friend joined the Faculty of Science at a university in Europe while your uncle went to South Africa to start a new life.

Losing my oldest son was like losing my right arm.

Your grandfather was grieving too.

He used to say

Is this

> the new garden,
>
> the new law,
>
> the new traditions
>
> > for which we have sacrificed
> >
> > so much?

After my oldest son left the motherland I focused on my younger son and my two daughters. I helped them complete their education and in that process I learnt that I was educating myself. I realized that what I had not learnt from my parents, I was learning from my children and I became aware that

> every son teaches his father
>
> every daughter teaches her mother
>
> and

every new generation teaches the older generation. They show us new paths which lead to new destinations. They make us see life through their eyes. My own thirst for knowledge was quenched through the education of my children.

In spite of the storms and strong winds that were destroying the garden, there were a lonely few who protected the plants of honesty, justice and liberty with their dear lives. Their efforts were, however, fruitless.

Before democratic rule had an opportunity to gain strength from its people, it was toppled by the dictatorship.

Before the institutions of human rights were fully established, autocratic systems took over.

Before the masses had fully recovered from the tornado of religious fanaticism,

> they were hit by the earthquake of an oppressive regime.

People on the streets were shocked
> because their
> tongues were slashed,
> lips sealed
> and
> voices silenced.

They were not allowed to express their opinions and feelings on the radio, television, or newspapers. They felt chained and suffocated in their own homes.

At that turning point both of my daughters spoke out against the oppression. One fought for human rights and the other for women's rights. One proved that the office workers, the farmers and the factory workers were denied their self-respect and the other showed that women had become second class citizens. They were neither given their due rights in mosques or in parliament. In spite of their talent, ability and character they were not allowed to be leaders.

People in power could not tolerate such criticism. They declared my daughters to be traitors and dismissed them from their jobs. Within no time, a doctor and a professor became jobless.

They contacted their older brother in South Africa and asked his opinion. He said it was not worthwhile living in a motherland that does not respect her children and citizens. So my daughters left; one went to Western Europe and the other to North America. The women who were insulted and rejected by their own people were welcomed by a different motherland. They were given jobs, and respected by the people.

When my daughters left, I felt as if I had lost my left arm. I cried so long that there were no tears left in my eyes.

For the next few years there was only your younger uncle at home. When he went to university, that left only your grandfather and myself at home. We felt lonely and sad. The house felt like a graveyard.

Your grandfather took his retirement and then had the time then to open the windows of his past. He reminisced about his old home, old homeland, old friends. His dreams were as wrinkled as his face.

He would stare into space all day long and would tell his son that it was his duty to take care of his new homeland because people had sacrificed so much to acquire that homeland. Your uncle was so taken by his father's advice that he joined the army.

He wanted to protect his motherland.

He wanted to look after the garden so that the flowers, birds and plants were not attacked and ruined by alien forces.

For a while he was positioned on the border of Kashmir, the motherland where his ancestors lived generations ago,

the motherland whose heart has been divided into two,

the motherland who was unaware of his future.

He was surprised that the natives of Kashmir were never asked about their opinions and their desires.

He felt as if two grooms had been duelling for a bride, willing to kill each other in the process. Nobody thought of asking the bride which groom she preferred. Perhaps she did not like either one of them and wanted to live a free and independent life.

Once, your uncle came home for holidays and while listening to the radio, he heard some bad news. The sword of history had struck once again and this time it had separated the Eastern and the Western parts of the motherland.

The army was called, and your uncle had to leave at once. He was sent to the Eastern part with thousands of other soldiers. Those soldiers, who were trained to defend their country against the enemy, were ordered to open fire on their own brothers and sisters.

Thousands of soldiers obeyed the orders but your uncle refused. He was court-martialled and sent to jail.

The motherland was in a state of shock. Her heart, having been previously divided in two, was severed once again.

Whatever dream remained in the hearts of the children of the sacred land turned into yet another nightmare.

The saplings that had been planted in the new soil twenty-four years ago had grown to become large trees, but they yielded only bitter fruits. The caretakers of that garden wondered whether it was the seeds that were faulty or that the trees did not bear sweet fruits because they never received clean water, fresh air and enough sunshine. The plants did not receive the warmth and nurturing they deserved to grow to their full potential.

On that land, tall concrete statues of religious ideals that had been erected by the people and had stood for years untouched were now eaten away by linguistic and cultural conflicts, as white ants devour and cause the destruction of whole buildings. The structures crumbled to the ground.

The tragedy was that the people who were destroying the garden were not outsiders; they were themselves the children of the promised land, descended from the original caretakers.

When your uncle was released from jail, he was a changed man. He was resentful. He felt that his motherland was haunted by military ghosts. He was angry that his love, his honesty, his integrity and loyalty were questioned. He used to say that his loyalty remained with the common people and his motherland and not with the army or the government. He used to say that the faces of generals and of political leaders change over time, but the people and the motherland are lasting entities.

Nobody listened to him.

Finally he, like his older brother, left his motherland late in the night and never returned.

Much later I discovered that he had become a businessman in the Middle East and had been learning Arabic from Arab bedouins.

My youngest child had now left his homeland. Your grandfather and I were all that remained of the family. We were now totally alone; our nest was empty. Our children, the young birds we had fed with our own milk and blood had flown away. Now there were only the two of us to console each other and cry on each other's shoulders. Although my brother's and sister's children took care of us, it was not the same. We painfully missed our own children.

I used to wonder why I was being punished. I was paying for a crime I had not committed, nor had the motherland, and she paid the same price as I. We did not deserve the punishment we were given.

It was just when all hope seemed lost, that a new chapter started in the history of this land. It was a new beginning and appeared to be nothing short of a miracle.

It was a movement of the populace.

Masses of people awakened.

The people crowded the streets.

Lips that had been sealed,

>opened once more.

Bruised, swollen tongues
>> began to sing.

The poor,
> the deprived,
>> the underprivileged,
>>> the minority groups,
>>>> started to protest.

They began to fight for their rights.

There was an atmosphere of hope, ambition and desire. It was a dream-like state that made us feel like we were floating in the air.

During that time, all the sons and daughters of the motherland who were living in exile and had adopted other motherlands, were invited back. They were reassured that their lives would be respected. Your aunt and uncles were planning to return. They felt optimistic in spite of the opposition expressed by their spouses and children. They realized that they were still bound to their mothers and motherlands with a delicate thread, remains of the umbilical cord.

But that promise was never fulfilled; it was a dream that never materialized. People's desires, their hopes and their wishes were small buds that were nipped before they could fully blossom. The military regime struck them like a bolt of lightening. It was as if a young princess of democracy was knocked unconscious, just as she was beginning to awaken. She lay in a state of paralysis from the drug given to her by religion and dictatorship.

It was but a few — the chosen, privileged leaders of our land — who wanted to keep the masses silenced. The underprivileged were induced into a state of deep sleep where they were harmless and defenceless against the evil rulers.

So your mother, your aunt and your uncles who had planned to return home, had to change their minds.

At that time I realized that a return to the homeland would never be possible. The mother and the motherland were now permanently separated from her children.

Your grandfather felt the anguish and the pain more deeply than any of us. He never did recover from this, his final crisis. One morning I found his cold, dead body lying next to mine when I awoke. His suffering had finally ended.

His eyes were still open. He was staring into space as if searching for the dream that had not yet been fulfilled. He had fantasized that the dream he had for his whole lifetime, would finally come true. Sadly though, his dream was throttled by cold, metallic, sadistic hands. Hands of oppression.

It was a sad and gloomy day when I informed my children of their father's death but not as sad as what followed. Not one of them could come for your grandfather's funeral. His body was bathed, carried and put into the ground for its final rest by strangers. That was my breaking-point. When I saw the faces of people I did not know at your grandfather's funeral, I could not bear the pain and fainted, falling to the ground.

Dear Child!

When I realized that my children could never come to see their mother again, I decided I must go to them. I ventured away from my homeland and visited my children and their families in all the various parts of the world. I bought a round-the-world ticket and packed my bags. It was the first time I had stepped into an aeroplane. That trip was a novel experience for me. It made me see the world through different eyes.

My first stopover was in Europe where I met my daughter and her family. I met your aunt, her husband and children in Paris. Her children did not know a word of Urdu or Punjabi and I did not know a word of French. My daughter was working as a psychiatrist in a French hospital while her husband was a university professor. He was a dignified man, very affectionate and kind towards me. I stayed with them in Paris for a few weeks and then I travelled with them across Europe by Eurorail. I saw England, Germany, Holland and the Scandinavian countries.

During that trip, I saw a lot and I learnt a lot.

For the first time in my life I saw

- gay men and lesbian women
- girls who had shaved their heads and boys who were wearing earrings
- labourers who were living in overcrowded, shabby rooms like sheep in a stable. They saved every penny they made and sent it to their mothers so that they could build a palace on their motherland.

And I saw bazaars where one could buy nan kababs, kulchay, kheer, halwa, gujraila, haleem, nihari and other Eastern delicacies.

In the end I visited the Scandinavian countries and saw the building where the geniuses of our time are awarded the Nobel Prize each year. I was pleasantly surprised to see the name of your uncle's friend in that list. Remember his old friend who was declared an atheist in his own country and whose house was attacked and burned to the ground by the students? He survived only because he was fortunate enough not to be at home that day.

I attended a function in Stockholm where I met a Sardarni. She said, "Aunty! Don't you recognize me?"

When I looked more closely with my old eyes I remembered her. As a child she would come to our home to play. She was the daughter of that Sardar who had hid us in his taxi and transported us to the railway station when we fled Amritsar.

"How are you, Sweetheart?" I asked.

"Aunty! I don't want to share the details, but since you left, we have not been happy. My two brothers lost their lives in the struggle of the Golden Temple and my father died from the shock of that news. I have left my motherland and am residing here now." I could feel the sadness in her eyes and in her voice.

When I returned to Paris I attended a European conference of psychiatrists where your aunt presented a paper on "Psychotherapy with Immigrants." I felt proud of my daughter. The experts and professors that attended the conference were very impressed by her lecture.

After finishing my tour of Europe, I flew to North America where I stayed with you, your mother and your family in Canada. I felt very spoiled. Your family took such great care of me and they took me to see the sights of North America. I visited Niagara Falls and Niagara-on-the-Lake in Canada. I went to the United States and got to see a studio in Hollywood, a Broadway play in New York and the casinos of Las Vegas. I saw the United Nations building in New York where the representatives of the First World decide the future of the masses of the Third World.

I also visited Washington D.C., a place where on one hand people are mugged, looted, raped and killed right in broad daylight and on the other hand, it is where the president of the United States resides. If he is not re-elected, he gracefully hands over the keys of the White House to the next elected president and is able to return to his home to become a university professor or a volunteer in a social welfare organization. He does not interfere with government affairs after he leaves office.

During my stay in North America I met quite a few lawyers, doctors, engineers, businessmen and other professionals who were physically in the West but their hearts and souls remained in the East, attached to their motherland with an invisible umbilical cord. It was not infrequent for them to feel nostalgic. I also met a number of Eastern writers, musicians and artists who were well respected in the West and had become a part of the mainstream of their adopted country.

It was during that visit that you had expressed a desire to come back to see me and find out about the lands of Punjab, Pakistan, Bangladesh and Kashmir and hear the story of your family and ancestors. You hoped it would broaden your professional and existential horizons and make you not only a better person but also an enriched journalist. I welcomed you with open arms and an open heart.

After visiting my daughters, I flew to South Africa to visit my older son. I stayed with your eldest uncle, his wife and children who lived in Durban. His children were surprised to know that their grandmother did not speak English and I was surprised to find out that my son was an active member of the Blacks' movement. He was fighting for their rights. He informed me that, like the caste system in India, people in South Africa were divided into Whites, Coloured, Indians and Blacks, based on the colour of their skin. Their skin colour had become a more important characteristic than their personalities.

My son had become the right-hand man to Nelson Mandela and he had joined a group that for a quarter of a century had worked diligently and made sacrifices in order to rescue him from captivity. Mandela, who had spent a quarter of a century in the isolation of prison on a deserted island, was like a gardener who was planting new trees which stood for freedom and civil rights and who hoped that Blacks would be able to vote one day and chose their own leader—a prime minister or a president.

I asked my son why he had joined the Blacks while he was not one of them. He reminded me that Gandhi was a citizen of South Africa before he came to India and started the movement for independence. The day India and Pakistan gained independence from British rule was the day we became indebted to South Africa. He felt that by joining the movement of liberation in South Africa, he was returning that historical favour.

When I finished my visit to South Africa and flew to Saudi Arabia to meet my youngest son, I wondered while sitting in the plane, how more unfortunate and unlucky a mother or a motherland can be than that her sons and daughters who had made significant contributions in the field of science, psychology, art and politics were condemned in their own home.

> They were considered
> atheists because of their scientific discoveries,
> pornographers because of their artistic creations
> and
> traitors because of their political views and involvements.
> For their accomplishments,
>  their brothers and sisters

were willing to stone them to death.

Dear Daughter!

The more excited and proud I was of my children when I visited them in Europe, North America and South Africa, the more ashamed and embarrassed I felt when I visited with my son in the Middle East.

My son had left the traditions of his family and ancestors behind and was living the life of a playboy. He drank and gambled and slept with women indiscriminately. He said, "Mom! Honesty, love and integrity are all mirages. Life is short and we should enjoy it to the maximum. We only live once." He had adopted a hedonistic lifestyle.

I was extremely anguished to see that Arabs treated Asians as people inferior to them and that they had become second class citizens in those countries.

I visited Mecca and the Holy Mosque in Medina and was surprised to see that the Prince of Arabia had built a palace taller than the house of God. When they invited him to join the sacred ceremony of changing *Ghilaf-e-Kabba* [Cover of Kabba], he was too drunk to join the devout Muslims and stumbled on the stairs. They had to continue the ceremony without him.

That day I realized why Arabs had invited American soldiers to fight for them in the Gulf War.

I was so heart-broken that, in spite of my son's insistence that I stay longer, I shortened my visit.

I returned to my motherland the next day. The journey had enlightened me in many ways, yet by the end, after my turbulent visit with my youngest son, I began to spit blood. I was extremely tired. It was difficult to endure such a long and painful journey at my stage of life.

It has been a blessing that you came to visit me. It gives me a chance to relieve the pressure from my chest. I am glad you are here, but the tragedy is that since I have returned, I am feeling unwell. I feel haunted by the past.

It is an illness
>that has swept
>
>my whole body
>
>my whole being.

It is an illness
>that has no name
>
>no treatment
>
>no remedy
>
>no solace.

It is an illness
>that haunts
>>every vein of my body
>>
>>every cell of my mind
>>
>>every depth of my soul.

It is an illness
>that has poisoned
>>my every hope
>>
>>my every desire
>>
>>my every prayer.

Since I have returned
>I have realized that

the conflicts of the people of our motherland are not any different than the conflicts of other motherlands.

Whether they are conflicts which are darkened by shadows of ignorance and poverty, or haunted by the ghosts of prejudice and hatred,

    these conflicts persevere

    they are felt by people all over the globe.

I have become aware that

    whether they are experienced by

        children or the elderly

        women or men

        the rich or the poor

    all passengers with conflict

    travel in the same boat.

    They are all children

    of the same mother,

    a mother,

    who has tears in her eyes

    when she looks at her children

    wherever they may be.

I have also realized that

    whether they are

        humans or animals

            birds or fish

    they are all children

        of Mother Earth

    and when the mother

        looks at their miseries

>                    she shudders with pain,
> sometimes we feel her shuddering
>                    as earthquakes
> and at other times
>             we experience her sighs
> as strong winds, storms and tornados.

I have come to the realization that as long as the sons and daughters of Punjab were living in their own home they had their identifies like Ravi and Satlaj, the rivers of Punjab; but when they moved to the four corners of the world they merged into the ocean of humanity.

> Who knows
>    what is gained
>             and what is lost
>                   when rivers
>                        descend into
>                             the depths of an ocean.

My Dear Daughter!

I am aware that these pains and sorrows are not only the pains and sorrows of this century. We will experience new tragedies in the twenty-first century when the children of Mother Earth will move to live on Venus and Mars and Mother Earth will become sad once again.

Darling!

When your grandfather died there was nobody to look after his body and bury him. It saddened me greatly. For this reason I have made a request in my will. When I die, I want to be cremated. My ashes should be divided in two parts. One part is to be buried next to your grandfather's grave and the other half is to be shared equally among my four children in the four corners of the world.

Dear Daughter!

    If my children cannot come to me then I must go closer to them.

    I wish them happiness and peace wherever they live. They are my gifts to life and the future of humanity.

    If I am sad, then it is my fate to be that way. I will find happiness only when I am close to them and in that journey I may have to turn into ashes.

## ROOTS - BRANCHES - FRUITS

"Families are like trees, you know. The way branches join the roots, the flowers and the fruits, families tie the past with the future."

A long pause. It was way past midnight. Only the slow whining noise of the powerful jet engines filled the thoughtful silence of the speakers.

"What do you think is the difference between cactuses and apple trees?"

"One bears fruits and the other thorns." There was muffled laughter, then another long pause.

"Migrations are difficult experiences. Immigrants are either lucky or very unlucky.

The children of immigrants are very unusual . . . either they become artists or they lose their minds."

"Why?"

"Because they have to carry the burden of their traditions while facing the challenge of their environments. If they succeed they become artists...otherwise they become insane."

My co-travelers, who were from a different time zone, were engaged in a long discussion. Half-awake after the six-hour wait for the connecting flight at Heathrow, I could hear only parts of their conversations. After a while their voices too faded away in the distance.

I was flying from England to Canada to meet my three younger brothers whom I hadn't seen for years. Time, I thought, is a strange medium. It flows without any regard for age, race, colour or creed. Yet we seem to be able to take snapshots of it throughout our life. It seemed only yesterday that the four of us were growing up together in Peshawar. Today they are ten thousand miles away, living in Canada.

When I woke up, we were over Montreal, coming in to land at Mirabel Airport. After clearing Customs, I walked with my suitcase out through the doors into the main lobby. Mohammad was waiting for me. Wearing traditional Muslim dress and carrying prayer beads, he led the way to his car. During the long drive from the airport to his house we caught up on each other's news. When we reached the house, his wife Zubaida and their two teenage daughters, Zainab and Faiza were all waiting to greet me.

When I gave them the presents I had brought from Pakistan, my nieces became very excited. Faiza hugged me and said, "Thank you, Uncle."

"Shukrya TayaJan," Mohammad corrected her. He wanted her to speak in Urdu rather than in English. Faiza became silent, her face sullen.

It was supper time. After we finished our meal, we sat around the table talking. Then Mohammad, sitting at the head of the table, looked at his daughters and said, "It's time for evening prayers. Let's all pray together."

Zainab got up right away. Faiza on the other hand remained seated. In her mischievous tone she said, "Wait, Dad! I'm listening to Uncle. When we are finished talking, I will go for my prayers."

"You can come back after your prayers, Faiza," Mohammad was loud and firm.

Faiza, upset, left the room.

The next morning, Mohammad arose early. I heard him knocking at the girls' door. "Get up, girls. It's time for morning prayers." It was Sunday morning and far too early to get up so I went back to sleep.

I woke up some time later. When I went downstairs for breakfast, I found the family in the midst of another confrontation. Mohammad was interrogating Faiza. "Why didn't you pray this morning?"

"I fell asleep, Dad." She was apologetic but defiant.

"Go and pray right now."

"After breakfast, Dad," she pleaded.

"Don't argue. Get up and say your prayers," Mohammad ordered. Faiza started to sob. She glanced in my direction but I couldn't intervene. Zubaida opened her mouth to protest but thought better of it. Faiza got up and left for her bedroom.

That evening, we sat together watching television. Faiza looked at the TV guide, got up and changed the channel to "The Benny Hill Show". Mohammad looked upset. "What a pervert. He always tells dirty jokes," he said as he got up and changed the channel. A show called "The Best of Saturday Night Live" came on. A skimpily-dressed young woman was delivering a monologue on female hygiene. Mohammad quickly turned to another channel but it featured the gyrating dances of a group of musicians and barely dressed models, to the tune of loud rock music. Mohammad flipped through the channels until he found a CBC documentary on teenage suicide. Satisfied with that offering, he came back to his sofa. After a few minutes Faiza got up and left, soon followed by her sister.

I was a quiet observer. My role as a guest made me reserve my comments, but I was curious. With a careful note of diplomacy I asked Mohammad, "So, what do you think of the girls?"

"Well, they are cute. Zainab is older . . . so she is sensible. Faiza though, is naughty. She does not listen." He paused for a while. Then he continued in his serious tone, "Brother, it's been hard. We have been living in this country for ten years. It didn't take me too long to realize that this environment is dead set against Islam. That's why we have to be more careful than we were back home. My daughters worry me sometimes. But I'm doing my best to help them understand their traditions and values. I'm sure they will grow up with Islamic values and be proud of their Pakistani heritage."

Without acknowledging him, I asked his wife, "How about you? What do you think, Zubaida?"

"I agree with him in principle. But it's hard on the girls. They want to have fun, but he won't let them. They want to be with their friends, but he makes them stay at home. He forces them to pray and recite Quran all the time. They get frustrated and cry sometimes. I feel for them. I think we should be a bit easier on them."

"If they deviate from the right path once, it will be hard to bring them back," Mohammad interjected.

"Mohammad, you were saying that this environment is against Islam. What did you mean by that?" I was curious about the West.

"This nation has gone astray. They have forgotten their religions. Nobody cares any more. They have long ago lost their respect for their elders and their love for youngsters. The children spend their childhood with baby sitters; the youth get into alcohol and drugs; adults struggle through their middle age with separations and divorces...and die of old age and loneliness in senior citizens' homes. That's no way to live. Even the animals in the zoo have a better life."

I was disturbed by the bleak picture he painted. But I

wanted to know more. "Then why is this nation progressing so fast? Why are they so prosperous?"

He remained silent for a few moments. "God is just being lenient with them. He is playing with the kite. He has relaxed his hold on the bobbin. He is just watching how far it will go. One day soon, they will run out of string. That day they will feel God's sudden jerk and their kite will tumble down from the sky and crash on the ground. Brother, they are getting closer to Doomsday."

"Then why are you living here?"

"Living here and trying to follow Islam is a continual uphill struggle."

I remained quiet. Again, I was a guest and I did not want to be too critical of his lifestyle. After all, it was his life. He had every right to live as he saw fit.

The next day I wandered around downtown. I saw McGill University, museums, art galleries, cathedrals and a host of other beautiful places. I went inside brightly coloured stores selling everything from hair ornaments to shoelaces. I was very impressed by Montreal. The clean wide roads, fast exotic cars, elegant buildings and churches with green copper domes, the clear, clean river through its heart, and the green parks with huge trees, all made me feel that I was in a different world. I must have walked for hours. I was lost in the corridors of the city. But I did not care. I followed my reflection glimmering from the shiny mirrored walls of the tall buildings along my aimless route. When I found my way again, I was on St. Catherine Street, moving along the sidewalk with crowds of bustling people. Men and women were walking hand in hand. Some were entering the stores while others were looking through the huge store windows, just window shopping. I found the French-Canadian women to be beautiful. They were well dressed and they seemed to look after their figures and appearances very well, unlike, I thought, the women of Pakistan. I remembered so many of them neglecting themselves after they got married or reached the age of thirty. I was exhausted when I got back to my brother's house.

I enjoyed being with Zainab and Faiza. They were very warm and affectionate.

They wanted to be open with me, but were afraid of their parents.

In the evening I was sitting in the family talking with Mohammad and Zubaida. Faiza came and sat down beside her mother. Then she looked at her father and asked hesitantly, "Daddy, our class is going on a camping trip. Can I go with them?"

"How many people are going?" Mohammad started the interrogation.

"Twenty students. Sixteen girls and four boys."

"You can't go. I won't let you go on a trip with boys. You will stay away from them."

"Why?" She looked confused.

"It's a sin to spend time with strange boys."

"But, Daddy! All my friends are going," she pleaded.

"I told you once and for all, you are not going," Mohammad shouted. Faiza looked crushed. Tears welled up in her eyes. She looked at her mother but did not get any support. She got up and left the room.

I was disturbed by the incident, but I did not express my reservations. We talked for the rest of the evening on subjects ranging from the general well-being of our relatives to the status of the sociopolitical mood in Pakistan. I went to bed quite late but I could not fall asleep for a long time. I thought it must be the time difference.

The next day I took my two nieces out for dinner. "Are you happy at home?" I asked them. My question was simple, but in return I received a flood of emotions, flames of rebellion.

"I'm fed up with Dad. I can't take any more of his lectures on Islam and Pakistan. If I could, I would run away from home right now," Faiza replied with a mixture of anger and despair.

"Why are you so angry?"

"We can't go out of our house; we can't take music classes in school; we can't go camping; we can't even talk freely on the phone, because Mom listens to our conversation on the extension; we can't watch the TV programs all our friends do; we can't go to our school socials." She took a breath and continued her tirade. "Dad orders me to pray and recite Quran every day. I don't understand Arabic, nor does he. I hate mumbling some nonsense no one can understand...."

Zainab sat listening to her sister's bitter tirade. "We are trapped here, Uncle. I'm so discouraged," she said sadly, "Faiza rebels. I go along, but its all pretense. I'm just waiting for my eighteenth birthday."

"What will happen on your eighteenth birthday?" I asked.

"I will leave home and never come back." She seemed to have weighed her decision carefully.

"But why on your eighteenth?"

"That's the legal age in Canada. Until then we are all minors. If we leave home before then, it will cause problems."

"What sort of problems?"

"One of my friends had to go to court to disown her parents. She now lives with her aunt and uncle, appointed by the court as her legal guardians."

"Disown parents?" I was shocked.

"Yes, Uncle! If parents can disown their children, why can't the children do the same to their parents? God didn't ask me to be born to my parents. If He did, I would have refused."

"How can you say that? Your parents love you and care about you very much."

"Maybe they do," Zainab replied, "but the way they show it is disgusting. Even the animals in the zoo get better treatment. We are lucky that at least we have each other." She pointed to Faiza and continued. "If we were not helping each other, we would have committed suicide by now."

I was deeply disturbed by her comments. "Do you want me to discuss it with your parents?" I was genuinely concerned, as I had become quite fond of them in such a short time.

"It would be like stopping a runaway train by throwing yourself in front of it."

"More like flying an elephant on a kite string," Faiza interjected.

"Water on a duck's back...just runs off," Zainab shot back, laughing ruefully.

I felt somewhat reassured by their humour. I laughed and

they joined in. Walking home from the restaurant, Zainab shared a secret. "You know, Uncle, We really like our Uncles Khalid and Sohail . . . but Daddy despises them. They are not even welcome at our house." I remained quiet. Although I was curious to know more, I did not want a confrontation with Mohammad who was waiting for us on the porch. Seeing him, the girls became quiet. I understood and changed the subject.

The next night, when the girls went to sleep, Mohammad took me out for a walk in his neighborhood. Not too far from his house there was a coffee and donut shop called Tim Horton's. We went in and pondered the long lists of offerings. Mohammad ordered tea and I opted for orange juice. We sat there sipping our drinks and chatting.

"I want to discuss something important with you," he said, looking troubled.

"What's that?"

"I'm worried about my daughters. Before they sink into the quicksand of sin, I want them married to some Muslim men of good family background. Listen, when you go back to Pakistan, keep your eyes open. If you find a couple of nice men, please let me know. I will bring them over here and arrange their weddings in accordance with Islamic traditions. We have a mosque here, so that won't be a problem."

"Have you discussed this with your daughters?"

"There is no need for that. We parents know best. They will appreciate our wisdom when they become older."

"But still, you can let them know your intentions."

"I'll talk to them after I select the men."

I tried to talk to him about his daughters' feelings, but he was staring off into the distance, focused on his plans. I remembered Zainab's remark, "Water on a duck's back...just runs off." I gave up, utterly frustrated. After a while we walked in silence back to his house.

The next morning I left for Newfoundland to meet my brother Khalid.

~ * ~

Khalid was waiting for me at the St. John's airport. Even at a distance I recognized him in his red shirt and black trousers. The two top buttons of his shirt were open, revealing a gold chain with a locket hanging on his hairy chest. After a warm welcome, he took me to his apartment complex in his shiny red Porsche.

We took the elevator to the top floor. His apartment was like a *Playboy* penthouse. Romantic posters with seductive pictures covered the walls. On his bedroom door hung a poster of an open door leading to a mysteriously lit dark room. The elegantly scripted message read, *"Wanted — overnight meaningful relationship"*. His living room was arranged tastefully with a big comfortable sofa set, a television and a stereo in one corner and a couple of oversized book shelves filled with colourful and interesting books.

When I commented on his place, he told me that women really loved his apartment. He said that they were willing to take off their clothes any time. I didn't believe him. I thought he was joking and I just laughed.

He had a large collection of albums. He turned his stereo

on and played some nice music for me as I browsed through his collection of books. One of the titles interested me, so I started to leaf through it. Khalid smiled when he saw me with that book and said that he referred to it on a regular basis. He commented that he did not know that I had any interest in the subject. I ignored him. I was amazed by its descriptions of the variation and number of positions two persons can enjoy in bed. Newfoundland was already beginning to be an educational experience.

In the evening he took me to Signal Hill. From the top of the hill I could see a vast landscape. The rugged hills, the brilliant hues of dusk on the ocean and the fresh cool air reminded me of the time I was living near the southern coast of Persia.

"The very first message across the Atlantic was sent from this hill. Now it's a historical site." Khalid gave me a brief history of the place.

"It's beautiful from here. A bit chilly though," I said to him as a sudden gust of wind blew in my face.

"It's always windy here. Being a small island surrounded by a huge ocean makes it even worse."

I looked around the hill for some time. I was completely taken by the exotic beauty of nature surrounding me. Some elegant trees nearby created a wonderfully lush effect. "What kind of trees are those?" I asked Khalid as I pointed toward some trees with silver-coloured bark.

"Those are silver birches. They look beautiful, especially in the fall."

"They look frail. It's amazing that they survive at all in this wind," I commented.

We were there for a long time. We talked about the island, its geography, its weather and a host of other interesting historical and cultural tidbits. After some time, we started to talk about women. I jokingly asked him, "Why didn't you ever get married, Khalid?"

He laughed, "Do you think I'm crazy? I don't want to dig my own grave. If I put shackles around my legs, I would still have more freedom."

"So you are saying that married people are all crazy?" I twisted his words.

He looked at me and smiled. "If they are not crazy, they are certainly naive. I can't see any reason why any man would ever want to get married in Canada."

"You mean there are good reasons for it in Pakistan?"

"You haven't got any choice there. If you can't have a woman without marrying her, then you are forced into it. That's your fate in a hypocritical society."

"Hypocritical—in what way?"

"It's a society where sex is considered dirty and masturbation a sin. Where meeting women is banned. Where as a rule, people marry perfect strangers in return for some tainted gold. Even after marriage, the wives spend months with their parents, and even when you are with your wife, you don't have any privacy, and you sleep with her in total darkness. There are millions of men who have been married for years but don't know what a naked body of a woman looks like. They are all waiting for the Day of Judgment when all of them will stand naked in front of God. He has promised them that only on that day they are going to have a revealing look at themselves and their women. Boy, are they ever suffering from delusions. But what can you expect but immaturity where there is no mutual respect?"

"Immature? You consider the whole nation to be immature?"

"And suffering from self deception. They are all exceptional cowards, and they feel proud of that. They have labeled their shortcomings as virtues. They get headaches from excessive masturbation but still won't accept that their sexual appetite is like any other desire, the only difference being is that its satisfaction is voluntary."

"What is the situation here?" I wanted to shift his focus.

Khalid smiled, "If you meet a beautiful woman and tell her how charming she looks, she thanks you for your compliments. If you invite her to a movie or a dinner she either accepts your offer or excuses herself with a smile. If she accepts your invitation, she might freely come to your apartment. She is very open in her conversation. She doesn't lie about her age or demand wedding vows before she goes to bed with you. Sex is considered a private matter between two consenting adults, in which religion or law has very little say."

"There must be some reason people get married here."

"I don't know. God knows better. The only thing I know is that marriage is not considered to be a life sentence. If relationships get too strained, then unhappy couples are not ashamed to separate. Divorces have become socially acceptable. Even their religions have accepted that, albeit grudgingly."

"You don't seem to think much of religion, do you?"

"Religions are all illusions. Mirages in the desert. Instead of digging in the ground for water, their followers run for miles in fantastic anticipation. Their thirst grows intense and their bodies weaken. They start to hallucinate and die in the sandstorms, clinging to hope, claiming they are loved by God. Whether you talk about Judaism, Christianity, or Islam, they all misguide the simple and the poor. They are all ruthlessly destructive in their suppression of individual and social growth."

"But surely Islam is different." I felt defensive.

"Look at how Muslims live. Millions of them pray several times a day, but very few know the meaning of what they recite. When they fast, they eat more than usual afterwards and end up in hospital with peptic ulcers. Nobody gives Zakat. Those who do only pay a mere two and a half percent, of which there is no mention in Quran. They go for Haj when they are old and sick and hope that they die there. They slaughter millions of animals each year in the name of God after their pilgrimage to Mecca, only to let the carcasses rot in the desert. They mistreat their wives and find justification in Quran to beat them. They send children to the battlefronts to kill other Muslims in the name of Jihad, and so many other things . . ."

"But you are describing and criticizing Muslims, not Islam."

"What is Islam? Is it not the lifestyle of Muslims? We are not talking about the fictitious Islam written in some books and present only in people's imaginations."

I became quiet. After a while, we left Signal Hill for his apartment.

In the evening he took me to a night club. He told me that I should experience the city with my own eyes. I became quite excited.

We went to a club called *Stanley Steamer*. It was around nine in the evening, but there were dozens of people standing in line outside the club. We joined them in the line; everybody seemed to be happy and euphoric. I remembered long lines outside the cinema halls back home, where people fought each other for a couple of tickets.

"They don't fight?" I asked Khalid.

"Once you join the lovers, you don't fight," he replied as he winked at the girl standing in front of him. "Some people hit it off standing in the line waiting. Then they go home rather than to the club."

The line moved slowly. After about half an hour we were allowed in. There were hundreds of people inside, more women than men. The lights were turned low but the music was loud.

"There are five women for each man in this town!" Khalid had to shout to make himself heard.

"Muslims are allowed to have only four," I tried to reply. But my voice was drowned by the loud music.

We moved away from the dance floor and sat down at a table. A beautiful waitress came to take our order. Khalid ordered a glass of beer for himself and Coke for me.

"Come on, have a drink with me, in the name of the Lord," he teased me. "You might never get an opportunity like this. You don't know whether you're gonna go to heaven or hell. Even if you make it to heaven, you never know whether you will get any booze or not. We have the strongest drink in the country. Just one bottle of our Screech will raise the temperature of those rivers tenfold!"

I ignored him and kept quiet, waiting for my Coke.

I looked around, taking in the scene. There were beautiful women, fashionable clothes and a sense of excitement. I liked what I saw. Khalid spotted two women in the crowd. He whispered in my ear, "I know those two. I'll invite them over. I will take one and you take the other. Their warmth will melt the ice of your inhibitions."

"How will you approach them?" I was curious and a little embarrassed by his straightforwardness. I was envious of my younger brother. He seemed to be very experienced.

"Oh, that's not difficult. I know them well. When they wanted to go out with me, I was interested in some other women. Now I am free and available."

A flower seller came our way. Khalid called her to our table, gave her a five-dollar bill and told her to give a couple of roses to those two women. In a few minutes, they came to our table.

Khalid introduced them to me as Sharon and Daniela. Then he took Sharon with him to the dance floor, leaving me alone with Daniela. She had beautiful eyes. I felt nervous around such an attractive woman.

"Tell me something about yourself," I hesitantly asked.

"Well, I'm thirty-five and work as an assistant manager in a bank. I live alone. I was married once, but I left my husband after nine years together." She was very open in a matter of fact tone.

"Why did you leave him?"

"A few years into the marriage, the relationship turned

cold. I didn't enjoy his company any more, nor did I miss him when he was away. I felt empty and unfulfilled. We should have said good bye to each other a lot sooner, but I was insecure and financially dependent. I wanted to hold on to the marriage like a child trying to hold on to his ice cube — the more he squeezes the more it melts. Finally, it turns into water, and so did my marriage. Finally last year I said good bye."

"Weren't you sad leaving home?"

"Relieved, rather. We now live separately and meet each other on and off as acquaintances. Other than a sexual relationship, which didn't exist anyhow, our interactions have improved."

I smiled to myself. The waitress came to our table once again. "What would you like to drink?" Daniela asked me.

"Coke, please," I answered.

"Rum and coke?" she asked for clarification.

"No, just Coke. Thanks."

"Don't you drink at all?"

"No, I don't."

"But Khalid drinks."

"Yes, he is far ahead of me," I smiled.

"So you have one less vice." She tried to make me feel better. Changing the subject she asked me, "Are you married?"

"No."

"Do you have a girlfriend?"

"No."

"Then how do you live your life?" she asked in astonishment.

It appeared that she was asking me this the same way she

might inquire, if you do not cook at home or go to a restaurant, then how do you survive? I did not know what to say. How could I have told her that in Pakistan, millions of people have forgotten about their sexual feelings the same way senile people forget their way home.

"I am shy," was my excuse.

"You don't look shy." I blushed at her comment.

"Let's dance," she invited me.

"I have never danced in my life."

"Don't worry about it. Nobody really knows how to dance here. It's just a romantic exercise." She held my hand and proceeded toward the floor. I felt like a little boy holding someone's finger on the first day of school.

We danced to a few songs. Her smile, her perfume, the warmth of her body were driving my forty-five year old body into a frenzied ecstasy. I felt like a sleeping volcano about to explode. We danced to a slow song as well. She held me close and kissed my neck. My naïveté was obvious. My face was flushed with excitement and confusion. I am a doctor and have seen hundreds of women naked delivering their babies. But this interaction with Daniela was very different. I was convinced that she was quite ahead of me in romantic experience. I could have learned a lot from her.

After the dance she suggested, "You are a nice person. Let's go home." I was shocked. In Pakistan I would have thought, "What a whore!" But it sounded so natural and innocent coming from her.

"But, but... I came with Khalid," I stuttered.

"Oh, don't worry about him. He is with my friend. I will

drop you home later on." I couldn't say no. I was helpless. She called to Khalid and Sharon. "Khalid, I'm taking your brother home. He is an interesting man."

Khalid smiled, winked at me and said, "Have fun, kids."

Daniela's apartment was comfortable and nicely decorated. She turned on the stereo. Kenny Rogers was singing. She poured a glass of wine for herself and asked me, "What would you like to drink?"

"What do you suggest?"

"Orange juice."

"That would be fine. Thanks."

She had already accepted my abstinence from alcohol. I felt at ease. We talked for the longest time. She came close, kissing my hands and then my cheeks. I was a block of ice, sitting there completely frozen in fear. My experience with women to say the least was limited. Beyond formal relationships with relatives, distant interactions with nurses and casual encounters with the prostitutes beside the Badshahi mosque in Lahore, my contact with women was nil. I did not know how to spend an intimate evening with a lovely woman. I felt severely handicapped. Daniela seemed to be aware of that and somehow understood. She did not make fun of me. In the end she said, "I enjoy your company. You are more than welcome to stay overnight."

I blushed and sat there speechless, held back by my past. "Thank you," I said sincerely, "but I cannot". She drove me home. As I opened the door of her car to leave, she gave me a piece of paper with her phone number and said, "Call me when you are free. I would like to spend more time with you. Life is short and the best part is to spend it with someone nice. I like you but I don't really understand you." She kissed my cheek and said, "Good bye."

I stood in front of the apartment complex with that piece of paper in my hand.

I looked at it several times but the numbers were still there. Those few hours with her in her apartment were more precious than a lifetime in the libraries.

The elevator ride seemed to take forever. When I entered Khalid's apartment, he was not there. The next morning, the sound of his key in the door woke me up. Over breakfast, he said to me, "Daniela is a nice woman. Other women call her choosy. She was kind to you last night."

"How come?"

"God only knows. Women are like clouds, you know. Sometimes it is dry for weeks, but once it starts raining, it rains for days. And it always rains on the rivers, never on the deserts," he smiled.

"I don't know much about women," I said, acknowledging my ignorance.

"If you stayed here for a while you would learn. This is a nice and sincere island. Women here are very kind and generous."

"Did you ever fall in love, Khalid?"

"Love is a mirage, a child's dream. It doesn't have much of a place in an adult's life."

"Do women ever fall in love with you?"

"Yes, but I try to explain to them in the very beginning. If they are looking for a bourgeois life style with a husband, two point eight kids and a dog named Muffin, they are wasting their time with me. I don't want to put chains on them or on myself. If they don't like my way of thinking, they don't need to get involved with me. That's why quite a few women are my friends and not my lovers."

It was an interesting experience to be around Khalid. I learned much from him in those few days. But I had a confirmed ticket to Toronto.

~ * ~

Sohail was anxiously pacing up and down in front of the luggage claims area at Pearson International airport. We had not seen each other for a long time. I ran toward him and hugged him. He hugged me back, a little hesitantly, I thought.

"Men don't hug men here," he whispered.

"Why not?"

"People may think that we are homosexuals."

"Why did you hug me then?"

"I don't care what other people think. I just wanted to let you know for your information."

When I arrived at their home, I met his wife Cathy, son Andrew and daughter Jennifer.

When I gave them their presents, Andrew said, "Thank you, Uncle", while Jennifer said, "Shukrya Tayajan."

Sohail smiled and said, "Andrew likes English while Jennifer prefers Urdu."

"That's great," I was pleased to find that both languages were used interchangeably at their home.

In the evening, Andrew suggested, "Dad, we should take

uncle to Yonge Street."

The whole city seemed to be ablaze in light. Highway 401 was full of traffic but moving fast. The twelve lanes with their wide curves seemed to cut a vast swath through the city. When we reached Yonge Street, Sohail parked the car and we all got out and started to walk. It was a fascinating street. I saw people of all colours and races walking on the side walks. On one side, people from different churches were distributing leaflets while on the other side, punks with wild coloured hair were dancing to the beat of a blind musician. In one corner there was a black man selling buttons and on the other a few ladies of the night soliciting. It was a very colourful atmosphere.

"Uncle, Yonge Street is the longest street in the world," Andrew said to me.

"And the CN tower is the tallest building in the world," Jennifer interjected as she pointed toward a beautiful tower.

"Did you know, Uncle, that it gets so windy up there, the top of the tower actually moves," Andrew explained. They actually designed it that way to withstand the wind. And they have these lasers to measure exactly how much the tower moves in each second." I was learning from the children.

"Uncle, Yonge Street reminds Daddy of Qissa Khan Bazaar of Peshawar," said Jennifer. "And Anarkali Bazaar of Lahore, where he used to buy sweets."

"Do you have something like that here? Where they sell Eastern sweets and snacks," I asked the children.

"Yes, we do."

They took me to Gerrard Street where I was surprised to

see a small Lahore in the middle of Toronto. Indian sweets and clothes, kebabs, cinema halls and women walking in saris gave me the distinct impression that I had never left Pakistan. We went into a restaurant for dinner. Cathy ordered some rice and curry which she ate with her fingers. I had never seen a white woman eating like that.

"You don't use a knife and fork?"

"Yes, but I learned a lot of Eastern customs from Sohail. This is one of them."

"And I learned a few things from Cathy." They were complementary to each other.

The next evening when I came home, Jennifer and Andrew were in a hurry, gulping down an early dinner so they could leave the house for the evening's activities.

"Where are you going, Andrew?" I asked.

"To play hockey. What did you play, Uncle, when you were young?"

"Cricket."

"I heard that England, West Indies and India are very good in that game."

"New Zealand plays quite well too."

"Nobody knows about cricket here. But they like baseball a lot."

"Well, we inherited cricket from the British."

"Don't they play cricket in Europe?"

"Hitler had legally banned it in Germany."

"Why?"

"He went to an opening ceremony and came back five days

later to ask who won. When he heard that the match was still in a draw he became very angry and ordered, 'No more cricket in Germany. Our time is too precious.'" Before Andrew left, I asked him, "How well do you play hockey?"

"Not too bad."

"He's on the school team. He plays well," Sohail praised him. "Where are you going, Jennifer?"

"For my piano lesson."

"She loves her music," Cathy said.

"Do you play piano yourself?" I asked Cathy.

"I used to play in the church when I was young. Now I help Jennifer sometimes. She has a lot more talent than I ever had."

After Jennifer left, I sat talking with Cathy and Sohail. I asked Cathy, "What do you think of religion?"

"I am not religious. But I'm not against religion either. Religions are our inheritance. If they can teach us to love and live happily, then we shouldn't avoid them. I don't believe in rituals though."

"I feel the same way. I was born in a Muslim family and Cathy in a Christian home, but we still get along fine. We don't have any fights or arguments about this," Sohail explained.

That evening, Sohail took me to see the University of Toronto. We strolled along Philosopher's Walk catching up on our lives. "All the intellectuals come here for a walk and to examine their lives," he joked.

"Sohail! Do you like Toronto?" I abruptly asked him.

"Very much. I'm a Canadian citizen now."

"Are you happy with your marriage?"

"Yes I am. Cathy is not only my wife, but a very good friend too."

"What about the language? Isn't that a problem?"

"It was in the beginning, but not any more. I learned French from Cathy and she is learning Urdu. English is our common language."

"Have many Pakistanis married Canadian women?"

"No."

"Why not?"

"For a number of reasons. Most of them don't respect women whole heartedly. They want to marry virgins but they want to sleep with every woman they meet."

"That's hypocrisy."

"Yes. An ethical rather than a religious hypocrisy."

"Do you see any long-term effect of this attitude?"

"Well I'm not a psychiatrist. But most of these marriages turn out to be boring.

"After living an exciting life, when they marry these young, conservative, naive virgins they want to forget about their past. They hide a big chunk of their lives from their wives and families. But when their daughters become teenagers, their past comes back to haunt them. Then they want to impose the strict rules of Pakistan. They get angry when they realize that they are stuck between the devil and the deep blue sea. They become misfits in the East as well as in the West. They end up very unhappy, even mentally ill in some cases."

"What do you think of your children?"

"They are darlings. Both are intelligent and well-behaved.

Andrew is good in hockey while Jennifer is talented in music. They both know English, French and Urdu. They are happy and caring. I am very proud of them."

"I found them charming too. Did you ever think about their future or their marriages?"

"I knew you were going to ask this question." Sohail smiled and continued, "Look, Brother, marriage is a personal decision. When my children grow up, they will be on their own. If they can't find partners in life, then they are not mature enough to marry, and if they can, then they don't need any help."

"Well said. My sentiments exactly."

"We can not live in the past. The branch that is not flexible enough breaks in strong winds."

When we came home, Cathy served us apple pie. Sohail had especially made some Halva for me — my favorite dessert.

I was going back home the next day. When I went upstairs to see the children, I overheard them talking.

"I'm writing this essay and I have a question."

"What?"

"What's the difference between a mosque and a church?"

"Music is a sin in one and a virtue in the other."

I burst out laughing. They came out and joined me downstairs to finish off the pie.

The next day Cathy, Sohail and the children came to the airport to say goodbye to me. My eyes were wet as I bade them farewell.

Flying back to Pakistan I was looking at all the snapshots of my nephew and nieces that I had taken during my stay in Canada.

I remembered the conversations on my way over.

"Immigrants' children are extraordinary..."

"What's the difference between cactuses and apple trees?"

I sat there thinking...

Translated by: Sohail and Raja.

## A MODERN YOUSAF'S MOTHER

*Yousaf was a famous figure in Middle Eastern religious mythology known to Christians as Joseph, through the Bible story of Joseph and the Coat of Many Colours. His brothers, jealous of Yousaf, threw him into a well to die. His grief-stricken father, the prophet Jacob, wept so much that he went blind. Meanwhile, Yousaf was rescued by a passing caravan and taken to Egypt. Yousaf was so charming and handsome that the mayor's wife Zulaikha fell in love with him and tried to seduce him. Yousaf was accused of having an affair with her and was sent to prison. In the prison he became popular for his ability to interpret his fellow prisoners' dreams. Eventually the king sent for Yousaf to interpret his dreams and offered him a high position in his court.*

She would sit in the sun on the roof of her house, and daydream the whole day long. Her dreams were like buds which had withered before they could bloom. This dreaming in the sun had weakened her eyes, and she feared that she, like Jacob, would lose her sight one day, waiting for her son to come home. If her son did one day return to her, then she would be able to recognize him only through her touch.

Along with the fading of her sight, she was also losing her physical strength; the silver in her hair and the aching in her joints were gaining momentum. Her diet, like her dreams, was becoming flavourless and insipid: she dare not enjoy the taste of salt for fear of her blood pressure rising, and she was forbidden to savour the sweetness of desserts due to her diabetes.

When she ventured to share her fears with her husband, he would give advice instead of listening; he counselled her to assist him with spreading the news of Allah and advised her to pay homage to Him. He would tell her, "Children are entrusted to us by Allah. He gives when He pleases, and He takes away when He so wishes. We must not put so much hope and expectation into our children."

She had stopped meeting with her friends and relatives. No longer did she attend the celebrations of birthdays and marriages, or the ceremonies for births and deaths. She passed her days feeling alone and abandoned, silently shedding tears. The wounds she suffered from the last gathering she had attended had not yet healed completely. She had overheard so many unkind words from neighbours that night:

- Look at her, she has grown old before her time!

- Her physical ailments have turned her hair completely grey!

- She and her husband share the same house, and yet it is as if they live in two separate worlds!

-The loss of her son has devoured her!

The memories of that last gathering tormented her. "If my son were here beside me now, he would surely put balm on my painful wounds," she thought to herself. Then she pondered awhile and thought, "Even when he was here, he never had the time. He never took the time away from his poetry and short stories to listen to the call of my heart. He preferred his friends to his own family."

She recalled that during one of his long absences, his poet friend had come to visit. He had asked, "Aunty, how are you feeling? Is there anything I can do for you while I am here?"

"My dear boy, I see you more than I see my own son. How lucky your mother is to have a son like you! Why does my son not live with his family the way that you do with yours?"

"Aunty, I am an ordinary poet, and I am destined to look after my family. Your son is an extraordinary man who has made all mankind his family. You should praise your son in the same way that his friends are proud of him!"

"Child, my son and I do not know how to talk to each other any more. Before he was even able to speak as a child, I knew all that he wanted to say, but now it is so different. We are worlds apart. Ever since he has started to compose poetry, wide rivers have come between us."

"Aunty, my mother and every other mother of a poet would say the same thing."

"But surely I shall perish in his absence!"

For a moment she had stood there silently thinking of her son. She then remembered his poem *He Will Never Return* and a crushing wave of pain rose in her heart.

Each Thursday she went to the tomb of Data Sahib* and gave alms, and once a year she would offer a black lamb as a sacrifice so that her son, the poet, her Yousaf, would be protected against the evil eye.

"Why don't you just get him married off?" so many of her friends would ask.

"He does not wish to get married," she would reply, and then change the subject.

He was a handsome man. Ever since his youth he had been chased by wayward ladies, the Zulaikhas, from his town. So many mothers wished to have him as their son-in-law; but those who knew him well would say that he did not believe in traditional relationships, and he wanted no part of marriage.

He was famous for his love affairs and his poetry since his college days. In his first published poem "Dedicated to an Unacquainted Sweetheart", he smashed the idols of patriotism, religion, colour and creed. His story "A Kiss" had created a scandal throughout the university. He tried to pave a new path for male and female relationships through his creative works. He had grown tired of the shadows, of the ghosts which had stifled human liberation. He wanted the walls of hypocrisy and moral extortion to come tumbling down. He wanted the night of union to be cherished and the night of separation to be banned forever. In his student days, the books by Faiz, Minto, and Faraz were his companions. Those who were more perceptive said that he was born in the wrong country, that some day his abilities would become public knowledge, and that his name would be known far and wide—either as a well-known writer or as a notorious poet.

"Son, you must keep away from women! Protect yourself, for they will put a spell on you!" his mother warned.

In the meantime, his father, who was an admirer of Iqbal, murmured, "India's poets, sculptors and short story writers...the minds of these are ridden by women."

And he would reply in Minto's words that if male pigeons sing when they see their doves, and stallions neigh when they see their mares, then what could be wrong with a man who composes poetry or writes short stories when he sees a woman?

One day, Yousaf packed his books and a few articles of clothing and prepared to leave his home, as he felt suffocated in that atmosphere.

"Mother, I am going to wander out into the world and search for myself."

"Oh my son, when will you return?"

"Dear Mother, the paths that we choose to follow in life are only one-way streets. You cannot make a U-turn once you are on a highway."

Twenty years passed, and for Yousaf's mother, every day seemed like a year and every night a century. She had not slept peacefully for even one night during these two decades; often she would awaken abruptly from her sleep from a dream about her lost son.

From time to time one of her son's friends would drop by and she would ask, "Have you heard from my son? What kind of a job does he have?"

"He is a student of psychology. He interprets the meaning of dreams for the people he meets," the friend would reply.

"Yes, but in the meantime, his own mother's golden dreams are turning into nightmares," she would respond forlornly.

"Aunty dear, do not worry. One day your son will be famous — a renowned poet!"

"No, Son, no-one really appreciates a poet. In this world, nobody values poetry and dreams. Ghalib was an esteemed poet, but people know he spent most of his life drunk and in debt."

Close by, Yousaf's father sat on his prayer rug writing to his poet son. "My boy, as well as the words of different poets, sometimes you should also read the words of Allah."

More time passed, and then one day Yousaf's friend came by with fifteen one-thousand rupee bills and said, "Aunty, Yousaf's publisher has sent this money for you. He says that Yousaf's books have started to sell."

"Many, many thanks to you, Son. Come and share our joy. Have something sweet. Eat these luddoos** and take these dried dates with you. I have been saving them for quite some time. They have been blessed with holy words from the Quran."

Yousaf's mother bought two black lambs at the market and presented them as an offering at the Shrine of Data Sahib. With the remaining fourteen-thousand rupees, she made arrangements for the addition of two new rooms to their home. When the first room was complete she hung her son's picture on one side of one wall of the room.

"Why don't you put the picture in the middle of the wall?" one of her friends asked.

"I have left room for his wife's photograph," she replied.

"But he does not want to get married."

"He will one day, when the phantom of poetry finally abandons him."

One night, Yousaf's mother woke up in a fright. She called to her husband for comfort. "I've had a nightmare."

"What is it?"

"I saw a vision of Yousaf. He was drenched in blood."

"For heavens sake, woman! Go back to sleep! It is midnight."

"No," she cried. "No!"

The following morning she went to the telegram office with her husband. They tried to place a telephone call to Yousaf's publisher, but there was no response so they sent a telegram.

The next evening, Yousaf's friend came to the door with bad news. "Your son has had a car accident. He is in the hospital."

On hearing the news, Yousaf's mother sank on to the floor on her knees; within the next few hours she seemed to age many years.

The police said that Yousaf's car had collided with a truck and had been completely wrecked. Only the licence plate, LUVING, remained undamaged.

All the relatives gathered at the family home. The next telegram that arrived said that Yousaf had died.

His mother made arrangements for his grave. Yousaf had always been close to his maternal grandmother, and so it was agreed that he would be buried beside her.

Yousaf's mother cried for two long days and two very long nights; her husband, in the meantime, recited the Quran and tried to console his wife with words from the Holy Scriptures. That gave her no solace.

A third telegram arrived the next day saying that her son's body would not be returned to their village. When the police investigated the accident, they found his driver's licence on which he had agreed to donate his body to medicine; his eyes and his heart specifically, were to be a gift to women.

Once the relatives had departed for their own homes, Yousaf's mother took to her bed and sank into a fitful sleep. She woke up in the middle of the night and went to the cemetery. Standing beside her son's grave, she gazed at length into the emptiness. Then she descended into the grave.

Lying there, she slept peacefully for the first night in twenty years, perhaps because she was lying next to her own mother, or because she had now accepted that her son would never return; or maybe it was because she was completely and utterly exhausted.

~ * ~

\* The shrine of a Muslim saint buried in Lahore, Pakistan.

\*\* A Pakistani sweet, often eaten on happy occasions.

## BIGAMY

The telegram was lying on the table. It read: "Susan, My brother died last Friday. Family suggested I marry my sister-in-law. I agreed. Date not decided. Hope you and Michael are well. Miss you. Saif."

"Bastard." I yelled. "How can he do this to me?"

I called my travel agent and booked the next flight to Pakistan. I found out that the minimum time I could spend there was a week because there were only weekly direct flights between Toronto and Lahore, Pakistan.

I sent a telegram to Saif informing him of my arrival. I had always wanted to visit India and Pakistan but I had never dreamt that I would be visiting Pakistan under these circumstances.

I consulted my lawyer who informed me that bigamy was illegal according to Canadian law. If Saif brought his second wife to Canada, he could be charged.

I arranged for two weeks' vacation from work and asked my sister to take care of Michael while I was gone. I told everybody that Saif's brother had died and I was going to Pakistan to offer him support. No one except my lawyer knew that Saif had decided to have a second wife. I did not know how to tell people. It was so bizarre, so absurd. It was craziness.

~ * ~

On the plane, I felt as if I was already in Pakistan. Everyone around me was speaking Urdu, Punjabi or Pashto. I could not understand a word they spoke. For the first time in my life I felt like a member of a minority and I could empathize with how new immigrants must feel when they don't understand the local language.

During the flight I was reminiscing about the past ten years of my life, spent with Saif. I remembered our get-togethers, our discussions, our ups and downs in the relationship and our dialogues about different aspects of life. Once he had said,

"Susan! I don't think you should marry me."

"Why not?"

"Because I know you more than you know me."

"What makes you say that?"

"Because I have lived in Canada for ten years and I know your culture, the culture you grew up in. But you have never lived in Pakistan. You don't know my culture."

"But I am marrying you, not your culture."

"My culture is a very important part of me. I have left my culture but my culture has not left me. You are marrying someone you don't fully know."

"Those sound like lame excuses. I think you are afraid of commitment. You are nervous and apprehensive about marrying someone who has already been married and who has a son."

"No, that's not true. You, Michael and I have been living together for more than a year and we are happy. Why do you feel you need a marriage certificate?"

"So that our living together becomes socially and legally accepted. Michael adores you. He is so attached to you. He loves you more than his biological father. His father was always drinking. He abused me and Michael for many years. Finally, when we met you, there was a sense of hope in our lives. It was as if God sent you to us. I think Michael would like you to adopt him."

"Okay. Then we will get married. You set the date, make the arrangements, and I will sign the papers. I love Michael and I love you and it does not matter to me whether we are legally married or not."

So we got married and Saif adopted Michael and we lived happily as a family. I was so used to living with an abusive husband that I could not believe that Saif could be so nice to me. It was hard for me to accept his affection. Small things used to surprise me. He would bring presents, take Michael for long walks in the park and make Pakistani sweets for us. He gave me back rubs when I was tired. It was wonderful. I had never been treated so well. I felt like a princess. But I was always apprehensive. I always believed deep down inside that it would not last. My close friends reassured me that because I had been an abused woman, I had lost faith in men and intimate relationships. They encouraged me to trust Saif whole-heartedly. He was a sensitive and caring man. They told me that my doubts and insecurities could turn into a self-fulfilling prophecy which could undermine the relationship and destroy it.

And then the words of the telegram echoed through my mind like sharp daggers that pierced my soul. It rocked my entire existence; it was my worst nightmare. The loving relationship we had built was crumbling to the ground as if struck suddenly by an earthquake.

~ * ~

Saif came to the airport to receive me. He looked sad. It seemed as if he had not slept for days. He had been crying. I told him I wanted to stay in a hotel. I did not want to be surrounded by dozens and dozens of people, members of an extended family who were mourning and grieving. Saif, respecting my wishes, put me up in a nice hotel.

After I recovered from the jet lag and got used to the overcrowded and dusty city, I met with Saif for dinner. I was angry and very hurt. I told him off.

"You bastard! How could you do this to me! You always told us that you loved us. You have been living with us for ten years and now you come home and decide to marry your sister-in-law just because your brother died. Have you always loved the woman? Did you have an affair with her? Have you always had fantasies of screwing her? You never had the courtesy or the decency to discuss it with me or ask my opinion. You just informed me as if I was your secretary or a neighbour. You've treated me like an acquaintance and not your wife. Don't you know I am your legally wedded wife and we live in a civilized society where we have only one spouse at a time? In Canada bigamy is illegal. If you ever brought your second wife to Canada then you would go to jail."

I don't remember what else I said in the heat of the moment. I was full of rage and I wanted to dump it all on him. He sat there quietly without saying a word. Finally I pushed him. "Don't you have anything to say?"

"No, not at this time. I don't think you will listen to me. You are angry."

"Damn right I'm angry!" I shouted. "Tell me right now. I can't waste any time. I am not here to play games. I want to know the truth, the whole truth. Did you have an affair with your sister-in-law?"

"I will come back tomorrow" Saif said, "when you are calmer."

Saif left and I cried all night long. I could not believe that my worst fears were indeed coming true. I could imagine any husband leaving his wife but I could not believe Saif would take a second wife. I was also surprised that Saif was not perturbed by my anger. He even thought it was justifiable. As I thought about the situation I began to understand my husband's motivations. Saif was always a determined man. He always knew what he wanted in his life. He never wasted time in idle discussions. He had his own beliefs and he did what he believed was right.

Maybe I should listen to him and try to understand his point of view, I said to myself. I was calm when he came to see me the next evening.

"Why are you marrying your sister-in-law?" I asked him in a more gentle tone.

"Marrying Surriya is no different than when I married you. When I met you, you were suffering. You had a young son that you loved and you wanted only the best for him, but you were married to an alcoholic who was abusive to both of you. I felt sympathetic. I wanted to rescue both of you from that hell. My love for you and Michael developed later on. You were dating me for a year and living with me for another year even when you were legally married to Jeff. At that time you were practising bigamy."

"But I was not sleeping with him when I moved in with you."

"That was later on. For the first year that you were dating me you were sleeping with both of us."

"But at that time I was not serious about you, and I was sleeping with him because I was scared of him."

"Listen, Susan! I am not asking you to explain yourself to me. You are an adult and you are ultimately responsible for your choices and the decisions you make. I am just sharing with you my point of view. If you get angry again then I won't be able to share my thoughts."

"I am sorry. Go ahead."

"My darling! You know that I love you and Michael dearly. I adore both of you. I was a lonely man when I met you and I am glad that you accepted me. Those ten years that I have spent with you and Michael have been the most fulfilling years of my life. But now I am at another junction. My brother Awais was killed. He was an honourable man. He was a school principal and one of the delinquent boys of his school belonged to a very rich family. He hardly studied but his family wanted him to pass his matriculation exam with distinction. His parents offered one lakh rupees to my brother as a bribe. Awais turned the offer down. He treated their son like all the other students in his class, and the boy failed. The following week, the results were announced and shortly thereafter my brother was killed.

"The whole school and the community have mourned his death. He was well-respected. The family were concerned for his wife and three young children. They wanted a guardian who could take care of the children. Susan! You have to realize that in third world countries there are no government and social agencies to help such families. To ensure the well-being and the education of the children, the elders of the family asked me to marry my sister-in-law, and I have agreed. This type of marriage is arranged primarily to adopt those three children the way you had asked me to adopt Michael."

"Would you be sleeping with you sister-in-law?"

"Susan! You are missing the point. Why are you so preoccupied with sex?"

"I hate the thought of competition."

"Anyhow the point is that I am marrying Surriya so that my nephew and nieces can have a half-decent life."

"How much time would you spend with them?"

"I can live six months in Canada and six months in Pakistan for a few years until these children grow older. Perhaps I will spend winters in Pakistan and summers in Canada."

"Saif, such an arrangement seems bizarre to me. Do you know any other man who has two wives?"

"Yes, my uncle has two wives."

"Can I meet his first wife?"

"That's no problem. But I thought you did not want to meet my family."

"For that, I'll make an exception."

"Okay. I will arrange it for tomorrow."

~ * ~

So I met Razia, Saif's uncle's first wife. She was a middle-aged lady with greying hair. She had a graceful look about her.

I spent the entire evening with her. She had a female servant, Nooran, who prepared dinner for us. During the dinner I asked her,

"You gave permission to your husband to have a second wife?"

"Yes, I did."

"Why was that?"

"I could not have any children and my husband loved children. He was the only son in his family. If I did not give him permission he would have divorced me and would have married the second wife. I could not have all of him without fulfilling his desire to have a family, so I had a choice. Either to lose him completely or let him marry again and be indebted to me for the rest of his life."

"Did he have children from his second marriage?"

"Yes, one son and one daughter."

"How do you feel about those children?"

"I have looked after them. I have baby-sat them. They were, after all, the children of my husband."

"What were your living arrangements?"

"We lived separately. He lived three days and nights with me and the same with his second wife. He alternated weekends. So we shared him equally."

"Did you feel jealous?"

"Once in a while. But I did not let jealousy rule my life. I could have left him but after twenty-five years I am glad I did not leave him. I still believe I was his first love."

"What kind of relationship have you had with his second wife?"

"We never get together. But if I get her on the phone while looking for my husband, we are civil to each other. We've never had any problem. She is glad that the children are fond of me. We share the husband and the children together."

"This is all so new to me. I have been living in the West, and I could have never imagined this arrangement. It is so very foreign to me."

"Susan! It all comes down to acceptance. If you care about someone you are willing to accept many things. And let me be honest. I have only a grade eight education. If I had left my husband I would have either been on the street prostituting myself or I would have starved to death. Instead, I am leading a respectable life. I have a roof over my head. The reality is that I am barren and in this society it is hard for a barren woman to live respectably. I have to share what I have. If I had had a university degree and I was financially independent like you, it might have been different."

"Do you know any woman who has two husbands?"

"My servant Nooran, she had two husbands. Would you like to talk to her?"

"Sure."

Surriya invited Nooran in and she had tea with us.

Nooran told me that she grew up in a tribe high up in the mountains. In those tribes there was a scarcity of women and to marry a woman one had to pay large amounts of money. Sometimes one man could not afford to marry, so two men would put their money together to marry the same woman. Nooran was very beautiful when she was young, so she demanded 30,000 rupees for her wedding, while the other women in her tribe were asking only 10,000 rupees. Since one person could not afford 30,000 rupees, two farmers put their life earnings together, 15,000 rupees each, to marry Nooran. She spent alternate weeks with each husband. She changed husbands after Friday prayers. Her husbands lived separately and had no direct connection with each other. Nooran lived like that for twenty years. She told me that in those tribes the children carried the mother's names rather than the father's.

Unfortunately there was an epidemic of cholera in that tribe. Hundreds of people died and both of Nooran's husbands fell prey to that epidemic. In her old age Nooran came to the city and started looking after Razia. Both older women were happy living in the same house.

I was intrigued, and amazed, listening to those stories.

~ * ~

When I was flying back to Toronto a week later on PIA I felt like a different woman. I had never thought that one week could affect someone so much.

On the day of Saif's wedding I sent him a telegram stating,

"Congratulations on your special day. My lawyer will be in touch with you soon."

## OPEN AND CLOSED DOORS

The first meeting with you appears to be from yesterday and yet it feels as if not merely years but centuries have passed. Some of the impressions from this period are still fresh in my mind, but some of the memories, after going through the turbulence of my heart, have faded.

After wading through the stream of youth and crossing the river of adolescence I finally reached the land of manhood, and it was then that I saw you coming down from the mount of alienation. When we came closer my heart was beating wildly, while beads of perspiration glistened on your forehead. Our tongues were mute. On seeing you closely I thought of a house in which secrecy had its abode, its doors and windows shut tightly to guard against intruders; when I looked at myself, I was reminded of that habitation where staleness and retention dwelled, and all of its doors and windows were open to let the fresh air circulate.

I opened all the doors of my being and invited you in, but your modesty and the uncertainty of your heart became a chain to your feet. After saying "I don't know you. I am so uncertain" you became quiet. I stood silent for a while, and then I moved on.

While I wandered along my path of loneliness, I met you at every crossroad. Whether it was you or your alter ego is difficult to know. Like the hues of a rainbow, you appeared in many faces around me. At one time I visualized you with long black hair, blue eyes and light skin, while at another time your hair was short, eyes dark and skin brown. Each time I saw you, there were subtle differences in your appearance. There were times that I was struck by your beauty, times that I was mesmerized by your friendly air. Sometimes you smiled at me, while on the other occasions you were quite serious. In each of your appearances I met you enthusiastically; however, the walls of formality stood firmly in the way. Many times you looked dubiously at me, wondering how I could keep so many doors of my being open to you, a behaviour that seemed so alien.

The sun of time continued to shine, and the ice of our relationship slowly began to melt. One afternoon we sat on the bank of a river for hours. You asked me many questions, and I told you the story of my past. You listened attentively as if analyzing each situation, and when I tried to reach the depths of your soul, you unlocked a couple of windows but kept the other entrances tightly shut. On each door that I came to, "Wait" was inscribed, and I returned smiling. Circumstances allowed me to meet your alter egos, and you perhaps met my alter egos. Separation, alternating with intimacy, followed the pattern of lunar cycles.

One evening you accepted the invitation to come to my home. You came toward me like a young frightened child who wades hesitantly into a cold pond. I offered you a glass of wine, but you insisted on a cup of tea, leery that the wine would open a few more windows and doors. You didn't stay long. I could not tell for sure if you really did not wish to stay, or if tradition, like a magnet, pulled you away from me. Without crossing the river of circumstances I could not reach you, so I, along with my alter egos swam the current of a changing tide hopeful that an unexpected change in force would bring us together.

Many suns rose and set; many moons appeared and disappeared, and like the changing face of the moon, you appeared to me. Then one night you discarded the veils of shame and modesty, and walking confidently, you entered through one door of my existence. We embraced in such a way that it was as if we had waited for that moment since the beginning of time. We touched, tasted and felt each other, and in the mirrors of one another's experiences we tried to make up our own beings. You opened a door of your being, and after entering through a door of my being, closed that door from inside. That night we were so intoxicated with each other's nearness that neither of us mentioned our alter egos. Before you left you tried to shut the other doors of my being, but you did not succeed.

You came again the following week, but your inner as well as outer person had changed. The colour of your skin, expressions of your face, and your emotional reactions were all different. I could not determine if it was you or one of your alter egos that had come to see me; I was, however, aware that this person had entered through a different door, and she too tried to close various doors, and I had to smile.

I kept on trying to open more doors and see more of your personality, while you went on closing the remaining entrances to my being. Many delicate moments came and went during these encounters; there were good times and there were bad. Some meetings tasted nectar, others bitter like gall.

One night, the moon had hidden itself behind the clouds, which spread themselves like mascara on the sky; it rained like an outburst of tears. We took each other in our arms to avert the chill of the evening air when suddenly the telephone rang. It was your alter ego. I was speechless. Neither could I say anything to her, nor could I speak to you. We hadn't yet come out of that storm when someone interrupted and knocked at yet another door. I didn't answer, but she had a key and unlocked the door. I found the two of you very similar; you both looked at one another with great intensity, and then back at me, ruminating. Suddenly you reached for a dagger tucked under the pillow and struck me in the back. The blow rendered me unconscious. I don't recall how long I remained in that state but do remember awakening to the soothing caress of your hand. One alter ego tenderly dressed my wounds while the other tore them open again. I could not determine which of the two you were, the healer, or the assassin. My whole being ached. You had embedded the dagger in such a place that I could have been left impotent forever; whether it was good luck or bad, I recovered. I wondered then how you and your alter ego really felt about me and my alter ego.

The framed pink heart in my room turned scarlet.

Springs turned into summers and many autumns embraced winters while we tried to loosen the knots of our relationship, our fingers bleeding in the process. The stronger our feelings became, the more our relations seemed like double-edged swords. The harder we tried to resolve our differences, the more entangled they became. At one point it felt as if I, you, my alter egos, and your alter egos were all members of the same family. Our pains and pleasures, our griefs and joys seemed to poison our relationship drop by drop, and our prejudices rode our beings like ghosts.

As time progressed our fingers lost their sharp talons, and yet our disputes became only worse. Our mutual bonds seemed to weaken, and were swept away by the torrents of jealousy and antagonism. Not only did the flowers lose their colours, but their thorns became more pronounced, stinging as the seasons changed.

One night you came to me raging in anger, you opened a new door, and closed all other doors behind which your alter egos stood. You threatened me with the termination of our relationship and then stormed out of my home. In the process of trying to close the doors of my being, many doors of your being opened, and the few glimpses that I could catch were enough to amaze me. It seemed that in the pursuit of one of my alter egos you had once again climbed the mount of alienation so that you might descend into the valley of affection for another being. All of your alter egos stood stunned behind each and every door.

In my room I looked at the framed heart which was changing its colour from scarlet to dark brown; I heard the mourning cry of blackening roses.

Centuries lapsed, and our sighs of anguish were voiced. It was then that you presented me with two alternatives: either you wanted to keep open only the doors to friendship, or you insisted on closing all other doors if you were to remain emotionally involved in the relationship. I demanded that all of the doors remain open.

We could neither agree nor disagree, and the train of time continued to click along its track. It stopped and started at various junctions allowing passengers to mount and dismount, while we never seemed to reach our destination. In all this time the bitterness toward each other increased and then subsided while we went on lamenting the fogging of the mirrors of our souls. It seemed as if you could never really get to know me completely, nor could I discover the mystery of your being. We both turned back halfway.

Today I feel the palpitations of my heart, uncertain if they have been provoked by fear or anticipation. Your eyes on the other hand twinkle like stars, a reflection that we could go beyond the halfway point. The moon of hope and the sun of experience shall be our guides.

The frame in my room is now blank; it awaits some eternal inscription.

Translated by: Sain Sucha

## COLOURFUL LABELS — EMPTY CANS

She gripped the steering wheel with all her might. Then she let go of it and wiped her sweaty palms on her pants, her self confidence in tatters.

For thirty-three year old Julie, the day had begun like any other. She had awoken in the early morning as the sunshine beamed brightly through her large bedroom window. The only dark clouds were those in her mind.

"Am I really successful?" As she lay in bed, she pondered this question and found herself thinking about her life.

"You are so beautiful."

"You are a very lucky woman."

"You have become Assistant Director at the age of thirty-three — the youngest person ever in that position."

"You're Superwoman, able to balance the responsibilities of a home along with the pressures of a challenging career."

"There's no limit to how far you can rise in the business."

She had listened to these comments for years and believed them. She was a successful woman . . . had everything a woman could desire. A big expensive house in the most fashionable area of town, a late model Porsche sports car, and a high-profile executive position in a company of sound reputation. She was planning for a future when she would replace her present boss upon his retirement and would be the first woman director of that organization. Yes, she had dreams and ambition without limit. On this sunny morning, it was easy to push back the nagging doubts and fears that occasionally surfaced.

After months of persuasion, Julie had finally convinced the director that she should and could represent him at the provincial conference. She was delighted by this honour; yet to her, it was merely one more accomplishment in a string of many. She spent hours preparing for the all-important opening address, researching details and organizing the concepts she would present. She purchased a new suit, sober yet feminine, from an upscale boutique. Her excellent taste was reflected in well-chosen accessories. She would look perfect for the occasion — as perfect as the presentation she would deliver.

She awoke again with a start. Lying there day-dreaming had cost her a precious half-hour. She sprang out of bed, showered, dressed and ran to her four-year-old son's room, calling out his name on the way. Instead of the brief cuddle they usually enjoyed, she picked him up and deposited him beside his clothes laid out for the day. Bewildered, he began to cry.

"Hurry up, Jonathan! I'm running late. Stop crying and get dressed. You need your breakfast and then we have to get to daycare."

"No," he sobbed, "I don't want to go."

"Get dressed! Get going!" she ordered and hurried downstairs to prepare breakfast. When she came up to get him, she found him back in bed, asleep. Shaking with anger, she gripped him by the arm and dragged him out of bed. Jonathan sobbed as she roughly got him into his clothes.

"You aren't helping Mummy at all," she cried out in despair. She sat him at the kitchen table and thrust a glass of milk into his hand. He was still crying. She quickly cleaned up the kitchen and got ready to leave. But Jonathan was dawdling over his breakfast and time was running out. Julie grabbed at his hardly-touched cereal bowl, startling Jonathan who, ducking in surprise, knocked it and his glass of milk all over her new suit. Shattered glass, milk and cereal littered the floor and

Julie lost her temper. She slapped him twice. Jonathan stopped crying and sat frozen in fear. Julie felt a sharp stab of remorse, for she had never before done such a thing.

The mess cleaned up, she drove Jonathan to his daycare in silence. For the first time she could remember, Jonathan got out of the car without a kiss, or even a good bye. Julie felt terrible. To make matters worse, when she arrived at the conference centre, she realized that she forgotten her briefcase with her cell phone and the notes for her presentation. She would have to wing it, as she was already late and there was no time to go back for them.

At the meeting, she collected herself as best she could and began her address. It was a disaster. She could not concentrate. As she groped for words, her carefully-prepared presentation remained inaccessible, filed somewhere far back in her mind. She stumbled, she mumbled. For the first time in her career, she doubted herself and began to question all the accolades of those around her.

Demoralized and fatigued after the day-long meeting, Julie left to pick up Jonathan, stopping on the way for a quick dash into the superstore to grab some groceries. As she pulled up in front of the daycare centre, one of the staff came running out to the car. Breathlessly, she told Julie that they had just rushed Jonathan to the hospital. He had been far too quiet all morning and by late afternoon, had begun to perspire and cough. They had taken his temperature and when they saw that he was running a high fever, they had felt they had to get him to hospital.

Julie sat there, filled with shame and self-reproach. What kind of mother slaps a sick child?

At the hospital, she felt relieved to learn that Jonathan would be alright. He was suffering from a flu virus that was going around. However, they wanted to keep him overnight for observation. She rushed to her little boy's bedside. "Hi, little man...how are you doing? I was so worried about you... Jonathan. I love you so much."

"Mummy, I love you too. Please stay with me tonight. I'm afraid. I hate this place." He looked small and frail and helpless.

Once again, Julie felt torn. She remembered her commitment to her social action club, of which she was president. She had to chair the annual general meeting and without her, there would be no meeting. What was she to do? It was seven o'clock and the meeting was at eight. After pacing back and forth in the hospital lobby for a time, she ran to her car and drove to the meeting. She parked but found she couldn't get out of the car. She sat there, trembling. Her doubts were becoming stronger and they were tearing her apart.

"Am I really successful?"

"Am I as beautiful as people say?"

"Just where am I going in life?"

"I had the Marriage of the Year featured in all the papers but it fell apart."

"I had a baby because my family wanted me to."

"I'm Assistant Director because I was the best candidate, or so they said."

"I have it all...or do I?"

"I totally blew it today...am I losing it?"

"They say I'm the perfect mother...but am I really?"

"Am I losing myself in the struggle?"

She was perplexed, agitated. Sweat trickled down her face. She sat there watching the dignitaries of the town strolling toward the entrance to the pavilion—doctors, engineers, lawyers, businessmen, men and women, all wearing genial smiles and fashionable clothes. She recognized the faces but realized she did not know who these charming people really were. And who was she?

"What's in all these cans...what's under the labels?" The question started to suffocate her.

She turned the key in the ignition. Her hands trembled as she gripped the steering wheel and turned out of the lot toward the hospital.

Translated by: Sohail & Linda

## DIGNIFIED DEATH CLINIC

William entered the clinic on a stretcher. The orderlies placed the stretcher on an examination table and quietly left. William felt the same sensation as he had when he took a flight to see his grandchildren. The airplane seemed to have landed.

He looked around him. Looking to his right and then to his left, he peered at the walls. Everywhere there were posters. Each was coloured with the shadows of death.

One proclaimed: *DEATH IS LIFE.*

Another read: *DEATH – A NEW BEGINNING.*

On another there was a picture of a dried leaf suspended in mid-air, with bold lettering: *ONLY THOSE SHOULD LIVE WHO WANT TO LIVE. FOR A DEATH WITH DIGNITY, CONSULT YOUR LOCAL DDC--DIGNIFIED DEATH CLINIC.*

At the bottom of the posters there were phone numbers and addresses.

William was half an hour early for his appointment. His private duty nurse Sharon accompanied him, holding his hand. He looked at her and asked, "May I have my digoxin pills?"

"You had one half an hour ago," Sharon replied.

"What about my urine pill?"

"You only take them on Mondays, Wednesdays and Fridays. Today is Saturday."

"You are very kind, Sharon." His eyes were moist with gratitude.

She smiled. "Most nurses are kind." She stroked his hand.

"Can you give me some water, please?" His throat was dry.

Sharon brought a glass of water and helped him to drink. She then wiped his lips with a hand towel.

"Why am I getting so forgetful?" he asked sadly.

"A lot of people at this age have difficulty remembering things," Sharon murmured diplomatically.

"I can no longer read or write. Even thinking has become difficult. Life is becoming a burden, for me and others too."

Sharon remained silent.

A nurse entered the waiting room. "Hi! My name is Anne. I'm a registered nurse in this clinic. What's your name?"

"William."

"Your date of birth?"

"I don't remember. I'm nearly seventy-five."

"Your address?"

"This city." He paused and then added, "And now this clinic."

"Social insurance number?"

"It is in my briefcase."

"Have you already written your will?"

"Yes. My lawyer has it."

"Are you insured?"

"It has been taken care of."

"Do you wish to send any final letter or telegram to any of your friends or relatives?"

"No thanks."

"Do you wish to inform any church?"

"No thanks."

"How many pills do you take daily?"

"One for my heart . . . one for my kidneys. . . and one for my liver. At least I think so."

"Do you receive any other form of treatment?"

"I get dialysis once every three months....is that right, Sharon?"

"How would you like to pay for the cost of your treatment?"

"My insurance company will look after that. What's your name, Nurse?"

"Anne." She paused for a moment and then looked directly into his eyes. "William, there are three ways to die here — in three minutes, in three hours or in three days. Which one would you prefer?"

"Before I answer that, tell me, what will they do with my body?"

"Whatever you want. You can be buried or cremated, or you can donate your body for scientific research."

"Can any part of my body be used for someone else?"

"Yes, your eyes."

"My blood group is O negative. I have heard it is relatively rare. Can that be used as well?"

"Sure, if you donate it."

"So after taking my eyes and blood, please cremate my body and throw the ashes into the Atlantic Ocean." He looked at the nurse and added, almost as an afterthought, "Does it make any difference if I die in three minutes or in three hours?"

"Yes. If you die in three hours, then your donations will be more useful."

"O.K. then I choose the three hour option."

"Did you live alone in your home?"

"Yes. But I had five private duty nurses. They spent one week each looking after me. These days I have Sharon with me."

"Would you like to have Sharon with you when you are dying?"

"Of course."

"O.K., William. You will have to excuse me for a few minutes. I will write all this information down, so you can sign it and make it all legal."

"Very well."

"When would you like to die?"

"Tomorrow evening."

"That's fine. William, there is a team of psychologists in this clinic, doing research on the subject of life and death. Would you mind if they asked you a few questions?"

"No, not at all. Send them in . . . and thanks. By the way, Nurse, what is your name?"

"Anne.

~ * ~

"Hello! My name is Robert." The young man then turned to introduce his companion. "And this is Angela." He continued as both of them sat down in front of William. "We are students in the psychology department. I hope you won't mind us asking you a few questions."

"Not at all. Please go ahead. You know, I taught philosophy for twenty years."

"Why do you wish to die?"

"Well, I am tired now. There was a time, when I was very energetic, enthusiastic and productive. Now life is a burden for me and I am a burden for others."

"Are you leaving an estate for your loved ones?"

"I wrote five books of philosophy over my lifetime. They are taught in several universities in Europe and North America. That is all I consider as my estate, my property."

"What did you find to be the most difficult thing in life?"

"Saying goodbye." William paused for a long time and then he continued. "But when I finally learned how to do it, it was time to say goodbye to life."

"Do you have any complaints about your life?"

"No, not at all."

"Thank you for talking to us."

"You are welcome."

~ * ~

"William, my name is Dr. Smith. Are you ready?"

"Yes. I am."

"We use two types of gas here. One makes you laugh and the other one makes you cry. Which one would you prefer?"

"Laughing gas, please." William smiled.

"We will take you to the other room for the anaesthesia. Sharon will be with you."

"That is just fine."

~ * ~

"Sharon, I feel tired. I am falling asleep. Sharon, give me a kiss. Good bye."

William's ashes were scattered on the waves of the Atlantic Ocean. Slowly they drifted down and settled into its depths.

A number of students were reading his books as they strolled along the shores of the Atlantic Ocean, unaware of the day's event. They were completely oblivious to the fate of the ashes.

Translated by: Sohail & Raja

## ISLAND

"Are your parents alive?"

"Yes."

"When was the last time you saw them?"

"Ten years ago."

"Do you have any brothers or sisters?"

"Yes, I do."

"When was the last time you saw them?"

"Seven years ago."

"Where did you see them?"

"In a supermarket."

"Do you have any friends?"

"No."

"Do you have a home?"

"No."

"So where do you live?"

"On the street."

"Do you have any source of income?"

"Not at all."

"Then how do you live?"

"I just live."

"For how long have you been living like this?"

"For twelve years."

"What do you want in life?"

"Nothing."

"What's your aim in life?"

"I have none."

"Can I arrange welfare for you?"

"No thanks."

"How about a place to live?"

"Don't bother."

"You must need money for food."

"No. I am fine."

"How can we help you?"

"Don't worry. I will be O.K."

My social worker felt helpless. She did not know what to say.

The police brought him to the hospital. He had been wandering around on the streets for weeks. He had no food, no shelter. He looked like a bag man. The weather too was getting cold. The winter had brought its first snowfall. The police became worried when they found him one night sleeping in a bus shelter. He had looked pale and weak. They thought he might freeze to death.

"Admit him, Doctor, and look after him," one of the police officers had suggested.

"Do you want to be admitted?" I asked him.

"No thanks. I am not sick."

I too felt helpless. The social worker called his parents. They came and took him home to look after him.

A few days later the police brought him back. We were facing the same dilemma again. The social worker called his sister this time. She came and took him home but he took off after a week.

The police brought him to the hospital once again. They believed he was crazy, and should be locked up in a psychiatric hospital for a few months. I did not agree. I thought he was an eccentric and a nonconformist. Society and the police could not tolerate him. The social worker this time sent him to a boarding home. The police threatened him that if he was found again loitering in the city streets, he would be put in jail. He smiled. He didn't care.

A few weeks later, on a Sunday morning, a young man was taking his son for a morning walk in the city park. The child saw something floating in the pond in the middle of the park. He asked his father, "What is that, Daddy?"

The young man recognized the object. It was a dead body floating upside down. He hurriedly called an ambulance from a nearby phone booth. The para-medics came and put the body in a body bag, placed it on a stretcher and took it away in their ambulance. The young man and his son accompanied them to the hospital's emergency department.

While I was examining the body, the child stood outside the room, bewildered. He looked at his father and squeezed his hand.

"Daddy," he said softly.

"What is it, my son?"

"Our teacher told us that if something is surrounded by water, it is called an island."

"That's true."

"Was this man an island, Dad?"

The young father picked up the child, smiled and gently hugged him.

Translated by: Sohail & Raja

## DEVTA

"Devta [1] has died."

The news spread through the town like wildfire. The smoke of hopelessness and uncertainty settled over everyone.

The people still vividly remembered that time in the past when their days of ease felt short and their nights of misery had begun to seem unending.

When the fibre of the population, from children, to strong men, to wise elders, had started to crumble from the inside:

their hearts had saddened;

the fire in their spirits had lost is glow;

the ash on their bodies had turned them to ghosts;

the fragrance of their characters had dissipated;

and their eyes had lost their lustre.

The whole town was enveloped by a cloud of gloom.

When people looked into the depths of their souls they saw only ashes -

They had no yearning nor any dream,

And they nurtured no storm in their life's stream,

There were no sparks, nor burning fire

Just a coat of ashes covering body and soul.

Then one day a stranger told the people that far from that town, at the foot of a hill, lived a Devta whose presence would' rekindle their torch of life.

The people travelled hundreds of miles until they reached the foot of the hill, where the dwellers from many other towns had gathered to receive the gift of renaissance from the Devta.

The Devta was a tall, long-haired man whose face glowed with a zest for living and whose eyes radiated warmth. He wore a long gown and his speech was eloquent, with a rich timbre. Devta greeted each man, woman and child with a smile, shook their hands, talked to them, embraced them and sent them back home with his blessings.

That nearness to him induced new hope, courage, strength and excitement in the people.

When the people returned to their town the ashes which had smouldered in their souls changed to embers. Each person brought back with him a new desire, dream, or devotion.

In this way the ashen faces of the people slowly began to beam with joy.

In the life of the people of that town the joyful days became longer and the sorrowful nights shorter.

After that, whenever the warmth in their souls diminished, they would go to the hill and pay a visit to Devta.

Then one day came the news that Devta was dead.

Large crowds of people went rushing to the mountain in whose bosom Devta had spent his days. There was no Devta to greet them; only his body awaited them. But before his death Devta had left a message for the people, written with his finger in the wet ground. The message read: "Every person among you is a Devta."

Translated: by Sain Sucha

---

[1]   In Hindi/Urdu, Devta means God, a demigod, a holy man or a good man.

# PEACE CLINICS
## A Bio-Fictional Essay

Ladies and Gentlemen,

I feel honoured to be invited as a keynote speaker to this International Peace Conference, to share my ideas and ideals about our Peace Clinics with this gathering of distinguished poets and philosophers, students and scholars, artists and mystics, reformers and revolutionaries, government officials and citizens of the world. Before I present my thoughts I want to make my political position clear. I am not a president or a prime minister, a king or a prince. I do not represent any government, religious or political party. I am a humanist psychotherapist and I am one member of a special team of volunteers and professionals that believes in peace and dreams of creating a peaceful world together. As Native Indian Chief Black Elk once said, "No great thing can be done by one person alone."

I feel honoured to be part of the team of therapists and research workers who are trying to understand the dynamics of contemporary political violence. They are not only trying to understand but also find ways to help people who became involved in this type of militancy, which causes hurt and pain to their families and communities. Alongside working on controlling such violence, we are also trying to find ways to prevent human suffering.

Although this initiative began as Peace Clinics it is evolving into the creation of peaceful communities, as more and more people are realizing that we are all involved directly or indirectly. We are all in the same boat, whether travelling on the upper privileged deck or in steerage. If the boat of humanity sinks, we will all be drowned. Fortunately, increasing numbers of volunteers as well as professionals are getting involved and I feel proud to be the one who had initiated such an initiative.

Many of you might be curious about how this project started and how it evolved to the international level in just a few years. Let me take you back a decade to 2001, when the world watched the horrific destruction of the twin towers on the morning of September 11th. That is the tragedy in which thousands of innocent men, women and children died. Many people feel that that event changed the world and started a series of episodes of contemporary political violence from Iraq to Afghanistan to Pakistan. Although such violence had been brewing underground for many years, the tragedy of 9/11 hurled it onto the international television screens and scarred the collective human psyche.

While that tragedy was unfolding at an international level, something very personal was unfolding in my life as a writer as well as a Canadian psychotherapist from a Muslim background. It was a strange coincidence that my book, *From Islam to Secular Humanism...A Philosophical Journey*, was published in September 2001 in Toronto and I had been invited for my first television interview on September 11.

Because of the New York tragedy, the television interview was postponed a week. During the phone-in following my interview, one of the callers mentioned that before me, she had not seen any Muslim publicly declaring that he was not a Muslim. I shared with her that I know many Muslims who are atheists, agnostics and humanists but they are still in the closet as they are afraid of the negative reactions of their families and communities. They are afraid of persecution, even execution. I shared with the caller that having reached the age of 50, I felt that the time had come for me to share my truth, hoping that it would encourage and inspire other humanists to share their truth so that we could have an open and honest public dialogue. During that dialogue, I shared my philosophy of secularism that includes freedom *of* religion as well as freedom *from* religion.

Alongside television interviews, I also participated in a number of radio interviews all over Canada. In one of those interviews, a caller asked me, "Doctor, you are a psychiatrist, can you tell me the psychology of those young men who attacked the Twin Towers?" I told the caller that it was an important question but I did not have the answer. I promised him that I would research the subject. That question and interview inspired me to study the biographies of Muslim suicide bombers and interviews of their family members.

While I was doing that research I received a call from Bill Peterson, the Chief of Police of Toronto. I was introduced to him when my publisher Bill Belfontaine wanted an endorsement for my book, The Myth of the Chosen One, about Javed Iqbal Mughal, a suspected Pakistani serial killer. Bill Peterson and I had an interesting dialogue about the similarities and differences between Pakistani and Canadian police officers. He wanted me to assess Mujahid Khan, a young Pakistani man who was arrested by ATT, the Anti-Terrorist Team.

When I asked my Psychiatrist in Chief Dr. Kwan, if Zahra, my Pakistani psychologist colleague, could accompany me to assess Mujahid Khan, Dr Kwan gave me his blessing. Interviewing Mujahid Khan was a fascinating experience.

The following week Zahra and I drove to Toronto and passed through many security hurdles before we could meet Mujahid Khan privately. I was expecting to meet a scared young man, but I met a tall handsome Pathan who was all smiles. He was wearing a typical shalwar, qamees and topi. He had a long black beard. He was thrilled to know that I had grown up in Peshawar, where his family was from, and spoke a little bit of Pushto.

Mujahid felt that he was wrongly accused. There was no bomb threat. He was just joking around with friends on the Internet talking about killing a few thousand Jews, Hindus and Americans in order to go to heaven, but the police took his jokes seriously.

As I interviewed him, his life story unfolded. He had grown up in Toronto and wanted to be a computer expert, but his father, Dr. Gazi Khan, lived in Pakistan and was a proud member of Al Qaeda. Dr. Gazi Khan was the right hand man of Dr. Fadl, who worked in the Red Cross Clinic in Peshawar. I told Mujahid, who had never been to Peshawar, that I had studied in Khyber Medical College which was only a few miles from the clinic where his father worked. Mujahid was very convinced that Al Qaeda was serving Muslims and that Osama bin Laden and Al Zawahiri were the true leaders of Muslims. He was not apologetic about his views.

When I told him that his views might get him into deep trouble in Toronto, he said, "Doctor, I do not give a damn what they think. They can do whatever they want. One thing these Canadians do not understand is that Muslims are not afraid of death."

When Zahra and I were driving back from Toronto to Whitby, Zahra told me that she was impressed by Mujahid's honesty and integrity. He had shared his truth and was not trying to make politically correct statements. Mujahid believed that members of Al Qaeda were trying to get rid of the warlords and were seeking to create a just and peaceful system in Afghanistan, a genuine Islamic state, as Mohammad had created in Arabia. They had destroyed the statues of Buddha because Mohammad had also destroyed such statues in Mecca.

When Chief Peterson asked my opinion, I told him that Mujahid did not suffer from Schizophrenia or Bipolar Disorder but had a religious ideology and fundamentalist personality. He was a sympathizer of Osama, although he did not have any plans to kill any civilians. I warned the police that he was quite influenced by his father, who was an integral part of a militant organization.

In the next encounter, we were approached by the Ottawa Police and Hildy, my Jewish social worker colleague and I drove to Ottawa to assess Doreen, an Israeli journalist who was charged by the Canadian police for her involvement in target killing. Doreen was attending peace dialogues between Israeli and Palestinian leaders arranged by the Canadian government. She had a list of five Palestinian leaders that she wanted to kill. Police found *Revolt*, the political biography of Menachem Begin, in her apartment.

After helping the Canadian police with that case, we were approached by the Washington police to assess Hugo, a Cuban political activist, who was a Communist and was part of an international anti-imperialist movement. Anne, my nurse colleague, who is fluent in Spanish, and I flew to Washington to assess Hugo. I was impressed by his commitment to his cause and his reverence for Che Guevara. He was surprised that I had visited Santa Clara in Cuba to see Che's statue and museum.

After all those meetings I was approached by Bill Peterson to become part of their Anti-Terrorist Team. I suggested we make a new Peace Team and he agreed. After that discussion we created our first

Peace Clinic in which Hildy, our social worker, became the family therapist, Anne, our nurse, became the group therapist and Zahra, our psychologist, became the community therapist.

In our Peace Clinic, we created special programs of individual, family and group psychotherapy and developed two programs that became quite popular.

The first one was called "Meet Your Enemy", in which we introduced politically and religiously motivated militants to members of the community that they hated. It helped them overcome their feelings of dehumanization.

The second one was based on discussions of biographies of world revolutionaries. We chose four leaders: Nelson Mandela and De Klerk from South Africa and Yasser Arafat and Yitzak Rabin from the Middle East. We highlighted how these leaders started their political journey as part of an armed struggle but as they grew older and matured, their violent consciousness transformed into a peace consciousness and they gradually became ready to shake hands with their enemies and to create peaceful communities.

After the establishment of our Peace Clinic, Chief Peterson helped us connect with the police departments and forensic units all over North America. We started receiving referrals regarding people who were involved in killing or planning to kill innocent men, women and children. The services of our Peace Clinic rapidly increased in demand.

In the next few months we received invitations from other parts of the world. For example Dr. Zahir Anwer called from Calcutta to discuss Daler Khan, a Sikh who was an active member of the Khalistan movement. Dr Fernando called from Sri Lanka to discuss the Tamil Tigers, who were involved in armed nationalist struggles.

In a couple of years our Peace Team was travelling all over the world and training mental health professionals and police officers to establish their own Peace Clinics. In the last ten years we have created clinics in ten countries. They are located in Canada, America, England, France and Germany in the Western World and Pakistan, Sri Lanka, India, Saudi Arabia and Israel in the Eastern World. From this small beginning in ten countries we would like to start Peace Clinics in a hundred countries over the next 10 years. For that dream to come true we need motivated professionals and dedicated volunteers. So in this International Peace Conference I am extending an invitation to individuals and organizations as well as governments to support us in this worthwhile cause of creating Peace Clinics all over the world. If you want to know more about us and how these clinics operate, you can visit our website, www.peaceclinics.ca.

In today's presentation, I will share with you ten insights about the people we have been serving and ten highlights of our therapy methods so that you have an overview of our program. I hope that it will inspire you to work with us in the future and support our cause.

**TEN INSIGHTS**

Our clinical experience and research have shown us the following:

1. Most Muslim militants living in the East as well the West belong to Wahabi and Salafi sects of fundamentalist Islam.

2. Many of those Muslim fundamentalists follow the teachings of Abul Ala Maududi, Syed Qutb, Ibn e Tema and Ghazzali.

3. For every militant that was arrested and received treatment, there are many more who are contemplating involvement in such movements and are sympathizers of militant and political Islam.

4. These Muslim militants have been brainwashed by their cult leaders who have cultish personalities. For these Muslims, their religious identity is more important than their ethnic, racial or national identity.

5. In the non-Muslim and non-Arab world there are other young militants who are followers of other religions, like Christianity, Judaism, Hinduism, Sikhism, and even militant Buddhism. They are all ideologues who promote violence to support their political or religious cause.

6. Alongside religious fundamentalists, we also assessed and worked with many Communists who believe in armed struggle and were involved in killing civilians to create revolution. Many of them were followers of Marx and Mao, Lenin and Che Guevara, and were committed to their anti-imperialist cause, the way militant religious ideologues were committed to their religious cause.

7. Alongside committed Communists, we also did therapeutic work with dedicated nationalists, like Tamil Tigers, who believed in their nationalist armed struggle and were willing to take the lives of civilians for their political cause.

8. We discovered that many men and some women who were involved in militant movements had not only a fundamentalist ideology but also

a fundamentalist personality; they were self-righteous and believed that their truth was the final truth.

9. We also treated many soldiers of Western armies who suffered from Post Traumatic Stress Disorder as they regretted becoming part of an army that was fighting an unjust war in Iraq, Afghanistan and Pakistan and killing innocent men, women and children.

10. We are becoming aware of the influences of families and communities that teach and promote violence in their homes and schools for followers of other religious sects and national groups.

## TEN HIGHLIGHTS OF THERAPY, EDUCATION AND REHABILITATION PROGRAMS

1. We isolate the militant person from their group and cult for an extended period of time so that they cannot be influenced by their cult leader and other cult members.

2. We introduce religious militants to enlightened religious scholars who teach them that alongside fundamentalist and literal interpretations of scriptures there are also metaphorical and peaceful interpretations of scriptures.

3. We have special meetings called Meet Your Enemy. We invite members of rival groups and encourage them to have a dialogue so that they can put a human face to an abstract concept of "enemy" and realize that they are also human.

4. We help these young men and women to work through their grief in psychotherapy groups as many of them have lost a friend or a relative in earlier violent struggles.

5. We have lectures discussing the history of different political and religious movements in the world and how they transformed over time. These lectures focus on the impact of colonial powers on the psyche of those who were colonized and discuss the insights of Algerian psychiatrist Frantz Fanon who believed that de-colonization was a violent phenomenon. We discuss how the philosophy of Lenin was different than that of Tolstoy, and the teachings of Gandhi differed from those of Fidel Castro.

6. We offer workshops discussing the biographies of various political leaders like Nelson Mandela and Yitzak Rabin, highlighting that they started their political careers believing in armed struggle and violence; but after gaining political experience and wisdom, ended their careers as peaceful negotiators with their enemies — Mandela with De Klerk and Yitzak Rabin with Yasser Arafat.

7. There is a special focus on developing peace consciousness to promote the idea that killing innocent civilians is not accepted in any peaceful community and culture, whether by police, army or any revolutionary group.

8. We have groups coordinated by experienced politically conscious psychologists to promote critical thinking so that the young people can

read scriptures and books of their cult leaders with an objective and rational mind.

9. We have groups run by art therapists who promote creative imagination and ask these group members to draw, sketch, paint and sculpt as creative ways to express their anger, hostility, rage and desire for revenge.

10. We have guest lectures by reformers and community workers who teach how to develop a compassionate heart. They inspire these young men and women to do volunteer work to serve communities of their enemies and develop a peaceful bond with the members of that community.

In the end, let me share with you a letter from a young man that I received last week. We receive dozens of such letters every week. This letter adds a personal touch to the peace philosophy we are promoting and teaching in our Peace Clinics.

*Dear Dr Khizr,*

*When I first met you three years ago, I had a violent consciousness. Your clinic helped me develop a peace consciousness. You and your colleagues helped me become aware of my self-righteous attitude and my fundamentalist personality. I used to follow a militant interpretation of Islam and considered Jihadis as my heroes. I was not aware that I was part of a religious cult. I was willing to give my life and take other people's innocent lives for my holy cause. Gradually, I realized that my holy cause was not that holy, as it was soaked in blood. There was a time I used to hate Hindus and Jews and wanted to kill as* many of them as I could. Your clinic helped me reform my attitude and become a peaceful person.

> Now I have made many Hindu and Jewish friends. They are members of what you call, "Family of my Heart." I want to thank you and your staff from the bottom of my heart. You not only saved my life but the lives of many more innocent people. Keep up the good work and keep on creating more Peace Clinics so that we can make a peaceful world together. Love ya.

Sincerely,

Mohammad Jalal

Dear Ladies and Gentlemen, Some of you might think that Peace Clinics are dreams but for us dreams are the seeds and when seeds find the fertile soil and the proper nurturing of sunshine and fresh air they become plants and grow to be fruitful trees. If our peace dreams become seeds in your heart and mind, they will bear fruit of Peace Clinics in your communities.

Some of you might think it might take a long time for our dream to come true. For those impatient ones I will tell you the story of an old man in India who was planting a mango tree in his backyard. His neighbour said to him, "Babaji, you are so old you might never see the fruits of this tree, as the mango tree takes seven years to bear fruit." Babaji smiled and gently said, "My grandchildren will enjoy those mangos." So we are planting seeds of peace in our violent environment hoping that our children and grandchildren will see the fruits. I hope you can join us in our dream of creating a peaceful world together.

## SACRED

As a part of her daily routine, Saima rose early to offer her morning prayers. After her prayers she went to the family room to recite the Holy Quran. When she reached up to take her Quran from the shelf, she was surprised to see that it was missing. She thought she might have left it in the basement but it was not there either. Then she went to her son's room and was shocked to discover that his Quran had also disappeared. Gradually it dawned on Saima that all the family's copies of the Quran had vanished.

For the past few weeks Saima had been perturbed by the almost daily television coverage of a minister in America who had announced that on September 11th, he would distribute a few hundred copies of the Quran so that people could burn them publicly. Saima had told her brother Abid that if that happened, the whole nation would be cursed. In that frame of mind, Saima had started to include in her prayers a petition to God for forgiveness of the world's sins.

Perplexed over the disappearance of all of the Qurans, Saima called her neighbour Sabira asking to borrow one of hers. When Sabira went to get it, she was shocked to discover that her Quran was also missing. When the two women panicked and called all their friends, they were informed that no copy of the Quran could be found anywhere.

"But why?" they wondered. Every body offered opinions:

"God has taken back all the Qurans."

"Allah cannot see His holy book insulted."

"God has promised to safeguard the Quran"

"We are all going to be cursed."

Suddenly Saima's brother ran into the house, out of breath. He gasped, "Sister, something terrible has happened."

"What's wrong?" Saima asked fearfully.

"When I went to pray, I found the mosque destroyed. Nothing left but ruins."

"What about other mosques?"

"They've all been demolished."

"Abid, something terrible happened here too. Our Qurans are missing. I called all my friends and theirs have disappeared as well."

"I think the Day of Judgment is coming."

"Abid, these are signs of a terrible curse."

Saima and Abid watched the evening news and were horrified to learn that on the morning of September 11th, all the heavenly books including the Quran, the Old Testament, the New Testament and the Geeta were missing, and all the houses of God including mosques, temples, churches and synagogues had been demolished. The entire world was plunged into a spiritual crisis. Religious leaders felt that perhaps all holy places had been cursed, as they had become the seats of violence and terror rather than peace and love.

For the next few weeks all the ordinary citizens of the world like Saima and Abid were anguished and lost. They felt emotionally and spiritually adrift without their holy books and places of worship. Such a situation forced the leaders of all nations and traditions to come together to seek a solution to this world crisis. They organized a conference with the goal of creating a new holy book. They asked people to offer their best books of wisdom literature for consideration. Leaders submitted the writings of their foremost poets, writers and philosophers. Such literature included sayings of Confucius, poems of

Kabir Das, Bullay Shah, William Blake and Walt Whitman, and speeches of Chief Seattle.

At the end of the conference it was decided that in the 21st century the world needed a new philosophy that would promote the idea of One God, One Religion, One World and One Humanity.

Following the conference, the media broadcast many programs covering the new and unified position on religion. In one program, a psychologist, a mystic and a humanist philosopher were invited to share their ideas.

The psychologist said that humans still need a God and a Holy Book as it fulfils a spiritual need.

The mystic stated that we no longer need a heavenly God. God is present inside all of us and speaks through our conscience.

The humanist philosopher shared that the future of humanity depends upon the development of self awareness, inner wisdom and social conscience in each individual.

It is possible that as humanity recovers it might transform this breakdown into a breakthrough and realize that all human beings are part of one human family as they are all children of Mother Earth.

## HISTORICAL MEETING

When Irfan invited me to attend a historical meeting, I had no idea that it would be such a memorable encounter. He did not give me any details as he wanted it to be a surprise. When I arrived at the airport, he was there to receive me. He took me to his home, we had dinner and I went to bed. The next morning he drove me to the meeting. He asked me to enjoy the day on my own as he had to take care of his responsibilities as one of the organizers of the event.

As I wandered around the huge hall, I was surprised at the length and breadth of the arrangements. On one side was an auditorium for lectures by intellectuals and scholars from all over the world, and on the other stood a number of pavilions that looked from a distance like cottages. Coming closer, I could see that each pavilion had a banner over the door. Rather than attending the lectures I chose to visit the pavilions.

The first pavilion was named 21st Century People. At first glance, that title seemed meaningless. I thought that all 7 billion people living on earth were 21st century people. But keeping that cynical thought to myself, I entered the pavilion where I found many men and women, some sitting reading books and others engaged in a passionate dialogue. I approached them to see what they were talking about and soon realized that they were discussing Stephen Hawking's recent book, *The Grand Design.*

The first person was saying, "After reading that book I realized that we are living in a multi-verse and not in a uni-verse. Knowing that completely changed my world-view."

The second person responded, "And I was amazed to read that the Big Bang Theory may not be correct and the question of how this universe was created might be an irrelevant question."

The third added, "I was fascinated with the concept of black holes. There have been many times when the whole universe disappeared into a black hole and after a while a completely new universe appeared. This cycle of death and re-birth of universes has been going on for a long time. Now we are forced to re-think our concept of the beginning and the end of time and the universe."

The fourth asked, "But why do you think millions of people refuse to accept these facts?"

The fifth responded, "Because they are not living in the 21st century."

At that moment I realized the significance of the title 21st Century People.

I came out of that pavilion and entered the one bearing a banner that said 20th Century People. The people there seemed more conservatively dressed than those in the 21st. century pavilion.

I came upon two women deep in discussion, the content of which seemed to indicate that they were psychotherapists. When they welcomed me and invited me to join their dialogue, I asked one of them what kind of psychotherapy she practised. She said, "I am a classical analyst. My orientation is Freudian. I ask my patients to lie down on the couch and free associate."

"How often do you see your patients?"

"For one hour, four or five times a week."

"For how long?"

"Four to six years."

"But I thought that most therapists have discarded that method. They have face to face dialogues with their patients and see them only once or twice a week."

"But I am a Freudian analyst and I see my patients the way Sigmund Freud used to see them."

At that moment I realized why she was a 20th century woman. She was one of those who lived in the 21st century physically but thought like a 20th century person. I did not want to offend her by saying that if Freud were alive today, even he would have modified his methods and practices.

Then I entered the next pavilion with a banner that said 19th Century People. When I asked an older man dressed in a traditional suit and a tie what he believed in, he said that he was a Classical Marxist. During our dialogue, when I stated that when Lenin put Marx's views into practice, it had limited results, he disagreed with me. He said that the problem lay in the faulty practice and not in the philosophy. His response reminded me of my Muslim friends who tell me that the problem is with Muslims, not Islam. When the Marxist asked my opinion, I shared that I had great respect for Karl Marx as a genius who made wonderful contributions to our understanding of the human condition. But after two centuries we know so much more and have gone beyond Marxist theories. Now we need to integrate his theory into new models.

When he pursued the subject I told him that Marx was preoccupied with class struggles and class analysis; but now we know that to understand the socio-economic and political condition of any community, country or culture, alongside the class struggles we also need to focus on ethnic, racial, gender, language, nationalistic and religious struggles. Since every community is unique, their struggles are also unique. The Classical Marxist smiled and said, "All those struggles might be important but the most important struggle is the class struggle." After that dialogue I shook hands with him and left the pavilion.

I wandered around the area for a while and realized that I did not have time to visit each pavilion, so I chose to enter the pavilion proclaiming itself 7th Century People. In that pavilion there were many orthodox Muslims with long unkempt beards, wearing caps and clutching tasbeeh [prayer beads]. They were arguing passionately with each other over the right way to offer prayers, fast, go to Hajj, offer zakat [charity], and whether Jihad meant purifying one's soul or declaring holy war on infidels. Many of them expressed satisfaction that in Afghanistan, followers of Osama bin Laden and Mullah Omar had destroyed the statues of Buddha because the true Islamic tradition was to destroy all statues and idols.

Then I entered another pavilion that said People of the Era Before Christ. In that pavilion there was a group of orthodox Jews with beards and long curly hair, wearing black hats and coats. Some of them were praying and rocking, while others were discussing the miracles of Moses and his encounters with Pharaoh. When I asked one of them about Jewish law, he said, "An eye for an eye." When I asked him whether he had heard the saying that if we followed the principle of an eye for an eye, half of the village would be blind, he thought I was being disrespectful to his philosophy and tradition. I apologized and left.

After that pavilion I was planning to go home but I saw two pavilions at a distance from the others. They were labeled 22nd and

23rd Century People. I thought I should meet those people before I left, so I entered the pavilion of the 22nd Century People.

When I talked to one of them he shared that he was born into an orthodox Muslim family. But when he became a teenager and studied science, psychology and philosophy, he said goodbye to all religions as they represented a tribal mentality. He realized that all human beings from diverse religions, nationalities, languages and cultures belong to one human family. He was pleased that more and more people all over the world are rejecting organized religions and realizing that humans are more important than age-old deities.

My last visit was to the pavilion of 23rd Century People. When I talked to one of the women there she told me that she was from an orthodox Jewish family who ate kosher food and believed in the Torah. They had a dream of going to Israel and seeing the land that was promised to the Jews according to the holy scriptures. But as she grew older and studied world history, she realized that most religions were more myths than realities and that holy books contained more fiction than facts. She realized that human beings were so arrogant and self-centered that they considered themselves the chosen people of God. She believed that human beings were irresponsible and had done a lot of damage to planet earth. One example was cutting down the rainforests; by doing that they had not only cut down the trees that provide us oxygen, but had also destroyed the habitat of thousands of species of animals, plants, birds and insects. She thought human beings should learn to live in harmony with their environment and consider animals and birds their brothers and sisters. She believed we were all children of Mother Earth. I was quite impressed by that woman who seemed to be a compassionate human being.

When I returned to Irfan's house I thanked him for inviting me to such an enlightening meeting. It had made me aware that although 7 billion individuals might be physically living in the 21st century, mentally they were living in different centuries.

The next day Irfan took me back to the airport. While we were waiting for my flight, he said, "Before I talk to someone, I ask myself, 'What century does this person live in mentally?' Once I figure that out, my communication with that person becomes easier." Before leaving, I thanked Irfan for organizing such a thought-provoking meeting that had included people from different centuries and cultures. Irfan said that knowing me, he was sure that I would enjoy such an experience. Flying back home I realized that it was a Historical Meeting in more than one way.

# TRANSLATIONS

## ADULT WOMAN

Why are people so nosy? Why do they like to gossip?
When she was married, they said so many things behind her back.
"She is proud of her husband's money."
"She is conceited because she is beautiful."
"She is arrogant because her husband loves her."
When her husband died, rather than decreasing, the gossip increased.
"Why does she laugh?"
"Why does she go out?"
"Why does she talk to strangers?"
"She is thirty years old. Why does she socialize with an eighteen-year-old boy?"
People whispered and the clouds of suspicion spread all over the city. When she witnessed, heard and experienced all that, she took a different turn in life. She suppressed all her physical and emotional needs. She covered herself so that nobody could see her. She started to pray regularly. She cut herself off from others and retreated into her own world. Even then people did not leave her alone. Her exterior remained the same, but inside she was changing. When the gossiping did not stop, she decided to leave her home and homeland and emigrate to a foreign country.

Since she was financially well off she bought a nice luxury apartment. The people in her building did not care who she was or what she did. But people from her own country, both men and women, lived there too. And they had the same attitude. They whispered,
"When did she come home last night?"
"Why does she not socialize?"

"Why is she so rude that she can't even say hello?"

She rarely went out, apart from to buy groceries or shop or see her doctor. She spent a lot of time alone. Some people saw her when she visited her mosque to offer prayers.

One day her doctor's office called repeatedly to remind her of her appointment but there was no answer. The doctor's secretary called the security office of the building as she had requested, should they not be able to reach her. When the security guard went to the 19th floor and opened the door he found her dead. She had had a fatal heart attack.

Even after her death the gossip continued. People were exclaiming to each other, "Why was a religious woman like her, who prayed regularly, watching an adult video before she died?"

Written by: Shakila Rafiq

Translated by: Khalid Sohail

## WHEN SHOULD I EXPECT YOU BACK?

I decided I had to sneak out of my home. In spite of being comfortable with my decision, my heart was racing with an unknown fear. Lost in my thoughts, I was just about to leave when my wife mysteriously appeared and asked the same old question, "When should I expect you back?"

I froze. She stood there with questioning eyes. I chose not to answer. As usual she remained calm while I became flustered. Even after leaving the house, it took me a long time to calm down.

It was a daily routine. Whenever I wanted to go out, she would ask me, "Where are you going?" I would be evasive at first, but when she insisted I answer, she would then respond with the dreaded question, "When should I expect you back?'

In the beginning of our marriage I considered it the routine question of a typical wife and did not give it much importance. But gradually that question stirred up an emotional reaction. It resonated in my ears. It bothered me even when I was alone. Leaving the house became a troublesome event. While I changed my clothes, I was already dreading that impending question. When she saw me getting ready to go out, she would disappear somewhere in the house but would mysteriously reappear the moment I was about to leave and ask me the same question. I started to feel as though she was taunting me. One day I got so upset at her query that I retorted, "How can I tell you when I will be home?"

She said quietly, "You must have some idea."

"No, I have no idea."

She became silent, but I could see her inner turmoil. Then I said with a touch of condescension, "You are well aware of Karachi's traffic and distances. How can I possibly tell you when I will be back?"

She nodded but I could see she was not happy with my answer. She said in a tentative way, "The circumstances in Karachi…"

Irritated, I snapped back, "Nothing unusual is happening. You don't have to worry."

"Why should I not worry about you?" She wouldn't leave it alone. I cut off the dialogue and stomped out of the house.

While I was at home she was relaxed and peaceful. But the moment she saw me getting ready to go out, I sensed her uneasiness and became nervous myself, which I think she could read in my facial expression. She would remain silent as if afraid of something. But she could not resist asking me the same old question at the moment of departure. Sometimes when I was late returning home I wanted to call her but the dread of her question stopped me. When I came in late, she wouldn't question me but I could see it in her face. To diffuse the tension I would say, "I had to visit many places, that is why…." She would be reassured and start warming up my dinner.

Every morning I tried to avoid her but I never succeeded. One morning she asked the same question in a different way: "Are you coming home right after work?" It caught me off guard. I stuttered and said, "Sure, if I have nothing else to do." Then in a fearful tone she suggested, "Then call me after work and let me know when…" I could not control myself and yelled, "Why do you keep on asking the same question?"

She looked puzzled.

I added, "I never ask you such a question."

"You should ask me too," she responded. "I would like it."

I stared at her, speechless. Then I said, "Look, you shouldn't upset people when they are going out." She kept quiet.

"Are you suspicious of me?" I asked.

"Why are you saying that? Why would I be suspicious of you?"

"Then why do you ask the same question every day?"

"It does not mean I do not trust you."

At that moment it seemed as if she wanted to say something more but could not. I got out of there quickly before she could ask her usual question.

Gradually, my wife's question became my obsession. To avoid it, I left the house as seldom as possible. I went out only when it was absolutely necessary. If I felt like visiting a friend, I thought of the agony of the question and gave up the idea. The more perturbed and disturbed I felt because of my surrender, the more peaceful and relaxed she looked. She sat calmly on the shore while I struggled in a turbulent sea. Whenever I faced her, I was afraid she would attack me with her question and I would shatter. I became afraid of my wife. I no longer found her charming. Whenever I sat close to her I was afraid I might get an electric shock if she touched me.

One Sunday I was feeling so suffocated at home that I felt I had to get out for some fresh air. My wife was in the kitchen preparing lunch. I wanted to sneak out but the moment I reached the door I heard her voice, "When should I expect you back?" At that moment I felt as if she was no longer a woman, and that she had transformed into a witch who constantly watched me. I looked at her, transfixed. And then a surge of anger overwhelmed me. I clenched my teeth and roared, "I will go wherever I want and I will come home whenever I want. Who the hell are you to...?"

She fled to the kitchen.

Ashamed and anguished, I gave up my plan to go out. I threw myself on the bed and lay there listening to the pounding of my heart.

A few days later, a friend from England came for a visit to Karachi. Because of my emotional state I avoided seeing him. However, he persisted in inviting me over, so I finally made up my mind to see him. As I went out the door to visit him, I realized that something had changed between my wife and myself. I said to her, "You did not ask me when I would be back."

She looked at me and said nothing. I volunteered the information, "I will be back in about an hour." She merely smiled.

I felt as if a heavy load had fallen from my shoulders.

Written by: Tahir Naqvi

Translated by: Khalid Sohail

# BIOGRAPHY

## MY FATHER'S BREAKDOWN OR BREAKTHROUGH?

When I was eight or nine years old I remember experiencing some tension between my parents. There were times they ignored each other. I remember a few times when my mother said,

"Go and tell your father dinner is ready."

Dad would say, "Go and tell your mother I am reading a book."

A few minutes later she would say

"Go and tell your father his food is getting cold."

And he would respond, "Go and tell your mother I am not hungry."

As a child I did not know what was wrong but intuitively I knew something was not right. Now I realize that they were two people who were locked in an arranged marriage. They had never dated, had not even seen each other before their marriage. Because they spoke the same language and belonged to the same culture, their friends and families believed they would be compatible.

Now when I look back at their marriage I realize that
- they lived in the same house but belonged to different worlds.
- they spoke the same language but could hardly communicate with each other
and
- they had the same ancestors but followed different traditions

My mother was the eldest and my father the youngest in his family

My mother was a religious, conservative and traditional housewife while my father was a non-traditional, agnostic mathematician.

He seemed to be from Mars and she from Venus.

Finally the family experienced a major crisis. It was the winter of 1962. My father used to go for long walks after dinner every night. Because of the cold weather he used to wrap a thick blanket around his body. On his return from an hour's walk, he used to knock gently on the door and call "Sohail" in an affectionate voice, and my mother would open the door for him.

On that cursed night when the nightmare of our family life began, my father returned from the walk earlier than usual, banged his fist on the door, and shouted, "Aisha, open the door!" My mother, who had never heard her name being called, especially in such a harsh way, was alarmed. Her sixth sense told her there was something terribly wrong.

She put her ear to the door. She could hear his heavy breathing, which confirmed her suspicion that something was not right. When she nervously opened the door she found my father staring into space. He looked quite different than the man who had left for his walk. Without acknowledging my mother, he rushed to the living room, threw his blanket on the chair and started pacing back and forth in the living room in front of the long mirror. My mother followed him and her eyes widened when she saw him pacing.

"Basit, are you okay?" She was concerned but also afraid.

"Paralysis, paralysis," he mumbled and began to examine his left arm and leg in front of the mirror.

"What happened?" my mother demanded.

"I am paralyzed. Paralyzed on my left side."

"But you look okay. You can walk." She tried to reassure him.

"You don't understand. I am paralyzed." He was irritated. Mom did not respond. She did not want to aggravate him further.

Dad paced back and forth all night long like a lion in a cage and kept on mumbling, "Paralyzed. I am paralyzed." Mom could see he was losing his mind but did not know what to say or do. Living in a foreign land she felt helpless. Her closest relative was three hundred miles away with no phone available on either side. She could not communicate with her neighbours who spoke Pushto while she spoke Punjabi. The only acquaintances in town were the Maqbool family who lived three miles away but there was no taxi available at that hour of the night. Mom started to pray under her breath.

Mom shared with me when I was older that she had been extremely worried about her two young children sleeping soundly in the next room, unaware of their father's condition. I was ten at that time and my sister Amber was five. "What if he loses control and hurts the children?" was the thought that sent a chill through her.

Mom stayed awake all night long, a night that felt like a century, watching her husband, a Masters-educated mathematician, a well-respected lecturer, pacing back and forth in front of a mirror trying to convince her that he was paralyzed on the left side of his body.

At dawn she made one more attempt. She said, "Basit, you must be tired by now. Have a little rest." She held his arm gently and guided him to his bed. He did not resist. After helping him lie down, she came to our room, woke me up from a deep sleep and said, "Sohail, your dad is not feeling well. I am going to get Maqbool sahib so that we can take him to the hospital. Why don't you sit close to him and keep an eye on him. I will come back as soon as possible." I rubbed my eyes, trying to wake up, not comprehending what she was saying and went to my father's room. He was restlessly tossing and turning in his bed. Mom put on her burqa and rushed outside. I had never seen my mom go outside the door alone. Her worried look and bloodshot eyes made me realize something was terribly wrong but I could not figure it out.

After an hour that felt like a decade, Mom returned with Maqbool sahib and babaji, the neighbourhood security guard. Dad was by then tossing and turning like a beached fish. Mom told me they were lucky to get a tonga at that hour in the morning. Maqbool sahib asked Dad to go with him to the hospital but Dad resisted. After some struggle they got him into the tonga and took him to the hospital. When I arrived at the hospital a couple of hours later, the nurses had tied him down in bed and the doctor was struggling to give him an injection to calm him down and he was shouting, "Don't tie me down! I am not hurting anyone!" Mom had arranged for a private room. She took me to a side room, made me sit in a window facing a garden and asked me to pray to God to help my dad. I remember crying and praying for my dad whom I loved very much. Whenever I wanted to see my dad the nurses refused to let me into his room. They told me he was dangerous. I did not believe them but I kept quiet.

The next day my maternal uncle and my grandmother flew into town after they received the telegram and took the whole family to Lahore to look after my dad.

In Lahore we stayed at my grandmother's home for a few months. My grandmother, my grandfather, three maternal aunts Hamida, Shaista, Faiza and my maternal uncle Ehsan all lived on the second floor. That floor had one living room, two bedrooms, one kitchen and one washroom. There was another family that lived on the first floor and the third floor was an open roof where both families slept under a starry sky in the summer time. To accommodate my sick father and all the relatives and friends who came to see him, my uncle transformed the living room into a bedroom. The first week the whole family was enthused to look after my father. None of them slept. But when they became exhausted and drained, they realized that their care plan was not realistic. So they set up four-hour shifts. In that way the nursing care of my father was divided into six daily shifts. That nursing care plan stayed in place for some months and during that time a number of experts were consulted.

The first consultation was with a medical doctor who was also a family friend. After interviewing my dad, he suggested that we take him to the mental asylum. Mom refused. She said as long as she was alive she would look after him at home. She believed mental asylums were for mental patients who had no hope of recovery and whose families had given up on them. She had heard of people who went to the asylum and never came back. She wanted to look after him as a devoted and dedicated wife.

Some religious relatives suggested consulting *peers* and *faqeers*, the spiritual healers. Dad, being an agnostic, did not believe in them but my mom consulted them. They listened to her story and gave her plates with verses from holy Quran written on them. Mom washed those plates and asked my dad to drink the holy water. To please her, he drank that water but there was no benefit. Rather than improving, his physical and mental health was getting worse.

As my dad's condition deteriorated, he started eating less and less and drinking more and more water. As he drank excessive amounts of water he had to go to the washroom quite frequently. When an internist was consulted he told my uncle that my dad suffered from Diabetes Insipidus, a condition in which the pituitary gland of the brain does not produce enough anti-diuretic hormone (ADH) and the person drinks excessive liquids and passes a lot of urine. The specialist prescribed some expensive injections that were not available in Pakistan. My uncle had to spend a lot of money to get them imported from England. Even those injections did not make my dad any better.

During those months of my dad's illness, my sister and I were not allowed to see him. The whole family was frightened of the unknown. In spite of everybody's discouragement I sneaked into his room a few times. My dad hugged and kissed me affectionately and mumbled a few words that I did not comprehend. I was never scared of him. I even encouraged my sister to sneak into his room but she was afraid of getting caught.

There were times my dad exhibited some strange and bizarre behaviour. At times he would stand on one spot for hours. At other times he stared into space or talked to himself. One night when I was following him upstairs he stopped on the last step and started to mumble. I realized he was talking to the stars. I listened to him for a couple of minutes and then said, "Dad, go ahead, let's go to bed." Without saying a word he moved on. Even at that time I was not scared of him. He was sick but he was never verbally abusive or physically violent. There were times when he shouted or screamed for no obvious reason but he did not hurt anybody. The family's biggest fear was that he might jump from the third floor in the middle of the night.

During his illness, Dad had a long talk with my mom one evening. He told her that he had done a lot of soul-searching and had come to the conclusion that he should resign from his job.

"Why do you want to do that?" Mom was alarmed.

"There is one thing I never shared with you. When I was appearing in my Master's exam, some of my friends came to see me the night before the exam and showed me the next day's paper. The more I think about that situation, the more guilty I feel. The only way for me to resolve the conflict is to resign. I am quite aware that it will hurt you and the children but it will clear my conscience. That is why I do not want to take that step and resign from my job at the college without your blessing."

Mom got up and left. She thought it was part of his illness and bizarre thinking.

As my dad's water intake increased to sixty glasses a day, someone suggested again that he see a psychiatrist. My uncle took him to see one. The psychiatrist suggested ECT, electroconvulsive therapy — shock treatment. My dad went once but then refused to go back. He said it made him feel worse, and also forgetful. I remember once my Uncle Ehsan and the tonga driver waited for him for nearly four hours but he refused to go. My dad told my uncle that his problem was spiritual, not mental.

When every traditional and non-traditional mode of treatment failed, the whole family became frustrated and desperate. There was a sense of resignation. I could feel a dead silence in the house. It felt like a hospital, like a morgue. As a ten-year-old boy I did not understand the dynamics but I could feel that the whole family was experiencing a living nightmare, a nightmare with no end in sight.

Then, when every treatment had failed and everybody had given up, something happened unexpectedly and mysteriously. One afternoon Dad's first cousin Lali showed up. She was always very fond of my dad although they did not see each other very often. After listening to the tragic story from my mom and seeing my dad suffer, she asked my mom to consult Shamsi sahib, a hydro therapist. She told my mom that Shamsi sahib had helped a number of incurable patients with his non-traditional method of treatment. Out of courtesy my mom did not disagree, but she did not agree either. At the end of the visit Lali enthusiastically asked once again, "Can you take Basit to see Shamsi sahib?"

"It is very hard to take him anywhere," Mom said in a tired voice.

"I will make a special request and see if Shamsi sahib will make a home visit."

In a couple of days Lali showed up with Shamsi sahib who was a tall, gracious, middle-aged, grey haired man, dressed in white and carrying a briefcase. Luckily my dad was in a good mood that day. He welcomed Lali and Shamsi sahib. After the formalities Shamsi sahib approached my dad.

"Lali told me you are not feeling well."

"I have been having a lot of pain in my back." He touched the area of his kidneys. "I drink nearly a hundred glasses of water every day and go to the washroom every half-hour."

Shamsi sahib opened his briefcase and took out a blue bottle full of water. He asked my dad to lie down on his back and requested my mom to give him a light massage and rub the blue bottle water on his back for a few minutes. Everybody was pleasantly surprised to see my dad cooperating. They were more surprised to see my dad feeling better. Within a few minutes the pain was relieved. Dad thanked Shamsi sahib and asked him about his method of treatment. Shamsi sahib explained that his treatment was based on the theory that all human illnesses were due to the deficiency of one of the colours of the sun's rays. Since there were seven colours in the rainbow, all illnesses were divided into seven categories. Shamsi sahib told my dad that his illness was due to the lack of light blue colour. He asked my dad to get either a couple of blue bottles or white bottles with blue plastic covers and after filling them with water to keep them in the sunlight from sunrise to sunset for two weeks and then take two teaspoons of that water three times a day for a few weeks. Dad readily agreed, which surprised the whole family.

While the family was arranging for blue bottles, Dad requested my mom once again to give him her blessing to resign from his job to relieve his guilt, as he wanted to become a high school teacher. My mom, knowing very well that it meant saying goodbye to a lifestyle that included a big house and private school education for her children, finally agreed, hoping that it would make him feel better. Dad was really excited that he could start a new life with a clear conscience.

In the next few weeks, while he was regularly drinking water from those blue bottles, he started to feel better. His water consumption decreased, his food intake increased and his bizarre behaviour went into the background. While he was recovering, there was also a personality transformation. This young college lecturer, who loved to wear suits and silk ties, shaved every day and spoke fluent English, started to lead a simple life. He ate simple foods and wore plain clothes. He grew a beard and started reading Quran for the first time. He developed a keen interest in the spiritual traditions of other religions. In one year, a materialistic man had transformed into a deeply religious person.

He resigned from the college and became a high school teacher. He never again became sick. All his students and colleagues held him in high esteem. They were impressed by his knowledge and wisdom. His illness remained a mystery for everybody for the rest of his life. The whole family believed he had had a nervous breakdown while he believed he had had a spiritual breakthrough. I sometimes wonder how much my father's condition played a role in my attempts to understand the mysteries of the mind and become a psychotherapist.

# ESSAYS

## Traditional Majority, Creative Minority

As a student of human psychology and a practicing psychotherapist I have developed a keen interest in the evolution of human mind in our personal and collective lives. Over the decades a number of psychologists have presented a number of interesting and fascinating theories about human personality. Based on my own professional and social experiences I have also been developing a theory of Traditional and Creative Personalities. In this essay I will share some of my concepts.

### NATURAL SELF

All children are born with their unique temperament and special gift that can be called their Natural Self. It is similar to the seed of a plant. Like a seed needs fertile soil, ample sunshine and fresh air to grow and become a healthy tree and bear fruits, human children also need loving, caring and compassionate homes, schools and communities to become healthy and happy, loving and peaceful adults. Those children who are exposed to neglect, abuse and violence turn into angry, bitter and violent adults who can become dangerous to themselves and to their communities.

### CONDITIONED AND CREATIVE SELF

By the time children become teenagers their Natural Self has transformed into two distinct selves:

A. Conditioned Self. It is the outcome of the social and cultural conditioning of their families and schools, communities and cultures. Conditioned Self is guided by should, have to and must.

B. Creative Self. It is the expression of the creative dimension of the personality and is guided by what people like to, want to and love to do.

## TRADITIONAL AND CREATIVE PERSONALITIES

Human personalities can be seen on a broad spectrum. On one end of the spectrum are people with Traditional Personalities who have well developed Conditioned Self and on the other end of the spectrum are people who have Creative Personalities who have well developed Creative Self. While many healthy, happy and peaceful people have discovered a balance between their Creative and Conditioned Self, there are others who are in conflict. Such a conflict can lead to anxiety, shame, guilt and depression, even breakdown. It happens when Creative Self wants to do those things that Conditioned Self considers wrong, bad and sinful.

## THREE SOURCES OF SOCIAL CONDITIONING

For the students of human psychology the questions arise:
What is right and what is wrong?
What is good and what is bad?
What is a sin and what is a virtue?
When we study different communities and cultures we realize that the values of right and wrong, good and bad and sin and virtue can come from three traditions.

## A. RELIGIOUS TRADITION

Some cultures have a strong religious tradition and people believe in gods, prophets, scriptures and religious leaders. Those religious leaders, whether priests or pundats, maulanas or rabbis, tell people what they should or should not do and if they do what they should not be doing then they would be committing a sin for which they would be punished in this world and the world hereafter. When religious people do not follow the dictates of their scriptures they feel guilty. In such cultures the authority of right and wrong rests with heavenly God and scriptures.

## B. LEGAL TRADITION

Those cultures that are secular have a legal tradition. They have constitutions that have laws for their citizens. Those laws guide people what they should or should not do. The people who break those laws are considered criminals, tried in courts and sent to jail. In secular cultures the authority of deciding right and wrong lies with humans not gods.

## C. HEALTH TRADITION

Some cultures that are health conscious have social traditions that are guided by doctors and nurses, psychologists and psychiatrists, scientists and health care experts. These professionals share their observations and results of their scientific experiments and research to guide people to adopt principles of healthy living. Those guidelines help people what they should or should not do to remain physically and mentally healthy. If people would not follow those guidelines they would get ill and sick and suffer.

In most communities in the world cultural traditions are a mixture of religious, legal and health traditions that evolve with time.

## TRADITIONAL MAJORITY / CREATIVE MINORITY

When we study human civilization we realize that in every community and culture there is a majority of traditional people and a minority of creative people. People with Traditional Personalities like to follow the rules and love to protect organizations and institutions whether social or cultural, religious or political. On the other hand people with Creative Personalities challenge authority. They like to break the rules they find irrational and unjust and challenge organizations and institutions they find restrictive and suffocating. Interestingly enough if we follow the evolution of any culture we will find that the creative minority of one century grows into the traditional majority of the next century and gives birth to a new creative minority which leads humanity to the next stage of evolution. It is fascinating to see how the villains of one generation become the heroes of the next generation.

## BIOGRAPHIES OF CREATIVE PERSONALITIES

When we study the biographies of Creative Personalities whether scientists or artists, poets or philosophers, reformers or revolutionaries, we find that they suffered because they were frequently in conflict with their traditional families, communities and cultures. It was not unusual for those traditional families and communities to appreciate the gifts and ideas of those creative people after a few decades, sometimes centuries, and shower them with rewards and awards. In the 20th century we saw a number of examples of that phenomenon. I will just share two such examples, one from the world of politics and the other from the worlds of science and religion.

Nelson Mandela of South Africa challenged the White Government and their racist laws and policies of apartheid. He was put in jail and declared a 'terrorist' but after spending a quarter of a century in jail he was released and seen as a 'freedom fighter'. He was awarded a Nobel Peace Prize for creating a multi-racial, multi-cultural democratic government in South Africa. The other example is of the Catholic Church that recognized the discoveries of Galileo, who was penalized and persecuted for three hundred years, because his findings about our universe were considered to be in conflict with the traditional and literal interpretations of the Bible.

In every community, Creative Personalities are trying to protect personal freedom. They believe that human beings have to be free to experience their creativity in their own unique way. Such creativity can be expressed in science as well as art, love as well as spirituality. Creative Personalities feel concerned that autocratic and restrictive religious and political institutions can kill the creative spark in people.

When we study different communities and cultures of the world, we can see that there are times in history when the traditional majority and creative minority are in conflict. Such conflict can lead to angry and bitter, even violent, confrontations. On the other hand there are times when the traditional majority and creative minority are in harmony and create a peaceful environment conducive to growth and evolution. That is the time when the creative minority appreciates that the traditional majority is securing and protecting the creative gifts of the past generations and the traditional majority appreciates that the creative minority is paving the way for future generations. It is a healthy balance between traditional majority and creative minority that is most productive and progressive. Such a balance is hard to achieve in families, communities and cultures but it is an ideal that we can strive to achieve.

## CLOSED AND OPEN SYSTEMS

It is evident from history that when any system becomes a closed system and does not grow with time and does not flow like a river, then it becomes stagnant like a pond and loses its freshness. On the other hand when a system remains open and is practiced by progressive and open-minded people it continues to grow and evolve producing wonderful fruits of love and labor. Life moves forwards not backwards. In any community and culture different people, whether traditional or creative, can follow their dreams and find their respective place in society but they need to respect the role of other people in creating a balanced life and community. With the passage of time we are realizing that human beings have unity in diversity and diversity in unity and such a realization is a key for future growth and evolution. I hope one day traditional majority and creative minority learn to respect and appreciate each other and work together for the common good of humanity. If humanity is like a boat then traditional majority is like an anchor and creative minority is like the sails. If humanity is like a tree then traditional majority is like the roots and creative minority is like branches and fruits. Throughout human history traditional majority has been representing our glorious past and creative minority has been an inspiration for our golden future.

## WRITERS AND SOCIAL CHANGE

*"To avoid criticism do nothing, say nothing, be nothing."*
— Elbert Hubbard

What role do writers play in social change? This question can be answered from a personal as well as a philosophical point of view.

Writers are fundamentally in search of truth. When they discover something significant, they want to share it with others in their creative writings. If they are successful in this sharing, their creations inspire their readers and help them get in touch with their own truth.

When poets create poems or fiction writers write short stories, there is no way for them to know how their writings will affect others or whether they will bring any social and political changes. The more gifted and talented the writers, the more they are intuitively in touch with the dynamics of their social environments. A few fortunate ones find a large audience to identify and relate to their creations. Fewer still become representatives of their generation or generations to come. In Urdu literature, this exalted place belongs to poets like Meer Taqi Meer, Asadullah Khan Ghalib and Faiz Ahmad Faiz and fiction writers like Saadat Hassan Minto, Quratul ain Haider and Abdullah Hussain. In English Literature poets like Walt Whitman and Ezra Pound and fiction writers like Virginia Woolf and Franz Kafka became representatives of their era.

Here is an important question though: When Ghalib was creating his poems and Kafka was writing his stories, were they consciously trying to bring social changes? Kafka actually left two of his novels for his best friend, Max Boyd to burn but Boyd published them posthumously because he felt that they were masterpieces.

When writers write to consciously create social changes, they become social activists. If their writings fulfill literary criteria then they can be both, writers as well as social activists though this can be a difficult balance.

On the whole, the worlds of creative writers and social activists are quite different. Creative writers, whether poets or novelists, playwrights or essayists, need to isolate themselves to nurture their creative imagination. Many creative personalities are shy and introverted. They need privacy and uninterrupted free time to create. They need to delve deep into the corners of their unconscious mind to give birth to their masterpieces. Many writers have a separate room in their home or a corner in the local library, where they 'deliver' their creations and those isolated corners become their labor rooms. The writings of creative writers can inspire social and political changes but many writers are not members of political parties as they cherish their creative freedom and do not want to follow the 'party line'. They want to write for all of humanity rather than just one political party or from a certain point of view.

In contrast, activists are members of social organizations and political parties attend their meetings and participate in the political process to change laws and social traditions. Such activists are usually extroverted, outgoing people who like to engage in heated dialogues and passionate debates. Many social and political activists are inspired by their own favorite writers, poets and philosophers.

Historically, during many social and political movements poets, philosophers and political activists worked together to bring social and political changes. Usually their roles were well defined like making a film in which writers, actors and directors each have a specific role. Sometimes a writer can also be an actor and a director but this is rare.

Some writers create poems and plays, essays and novels, and others write books about science and psychology, economics and political science, sociology and anthropology. Some like Karl Marx dreamt of social and political revolutions while others, like Charles Darwin, Sigmund Freud and Albert Einstein, broadened our existential horizons and helped us understand life and the universe around us. When people develop social consciousness i.e. awareness about the society and the social milieu they live in, it becomes easier for them to strive for desired social changes. Some writers strive to change people's attitudes while others strive to change the environment and circumstances they find themselves in and both efforts are intimately connected. When someone strives to change their society, they change themselves in the process and vice versa.

A study of the social and political changes of the 20$^{th}$ century shows us two distinct traditions that were inspired by gifted writers. The first tradition was of people who believed in the inevitability of armed struggle. Revolutionaries like Ho Chi Minh, Che Guevara and Fidel Castro were inspired by the writings of Vladimir Lenin, Mao Tse Tung and Karl Marx who believed that social change requires not shirking from aggression in a noble cause. They also believed that when confronted by an implacable opponent willing to practice violence, a peaceful struggle is not enough. They believed that peace can be achieved eventually through militant struggle. The other tradition was of people who believed in bringing social and political changes by peaceful means and did not believe in armed struggle. They were inspired by writers and reformers like Martin Luther King Jr., Mohandas Gandhi and Leo Tolstoy. Such writers believed that peaceful ends do not justify violent means. They were of the opinion that using violence to create peace was a dangerous proposition

Writers of different traditions share their truth in their writings hoping that personal and social truth will liberate humanity. They hope that truth will help human beings to decrease human suffering. Over the centuries writers have played a significant role in social change and human evolution. Fortunate are the communities and cultures that have writers who are not only entertaining but also enlightening, who are not only poetic but also philosophical, who have, not only hindsight, but also insight and foresight to lead the caravan of humanity towards a peaceful world, together.

# INTERVIEW

## CREATING A PEACEFUL WORLD TOGETHER

Dr. Khalid Sohail Interviewed by Syed Azeem

**AZEEM**: When did you leave Pakistan? When did you come to Canada and for how long you have been living in Toronto?

**SOHAIL**: I graduated from Khyber Medical College Peshawar Pakistan in 1974. After one year of internship in Medicine, Gynaecology and Obstetrics, I went to Iran. I stayed in Tehran for a few months and then moved to Hamadan for a year. I used to work in a children's hospital that was located just opposite to the tomb of the famous physician philosopher Avicenna. During that year I applied to different universities all over the world to do my residency in psychiatry. I was accepted in Ireland, New Zealand and Newfoundland, Canada. I chose Canada and did my four year residency training in psychiatry from 1977 to 1981. After receiving my Fellowship in psychiatry in 1982 and working for two years in New Brunswick, I moved to Ontario in 1984. I worked at Whitby Psychiatric Hospital for 10 years and then started my own Creative Psychotherapy Clinic. I have been working there since 1995.

**AZEEM**: You are a prolific writer. You have published more than twenty books in Urdu and English in the last couple of decades. What is the secret of your tremendous output?

**SOHAIL**: There are many significant factors. One factor is that I have lived alone for the last two decades. I have not carried on my shoulders the responsibilities of a traditional family. Many poets, writers and artists that I know spend a lot of time and energy looking after their children. After fulfilling those responsibilities they feel drained and exhausted, and have a difficult time creating anything. It is very difficult for them to balance their personal, professional and creative lives.

Over the years I have discovered a few things about my creative process. I am most creative in the mornings. So I have dedicated my Saturday, Sunday, Monday and Tuesday mornings for my creative work. On Mondays and Tuesdays I start my clinic after lunch.

A few years ago I wrote an article, "From Creative Rain to Creative Spring", in which I shared the dynamics of my creative journey. There was a time I used to receive creative rain and I would write a poem, a story or an essay and then there would be a dry period for months. Over the years that rain has transformed into a spring that flows in the depths of my being and now I write on a regular basis. When I am not doing some original writing I translate world literature into Urdu. Such translations help me in maintaining my creative mood. I also have regular meetings with my creative friends on Sunday afternoons and discuss ideas and writings. Those discussions are quite inspiring and creativo-genic. We add those writings on my website www.drsohail.com so that other creative friends who live in many parts of the world can read them too. I also contribute regularly to Urdu magazines in Pakistan and India and English magazines on the Internet. These publications keep me connected with the creative community all over the world. The Internet is such a wonderful medium.

The last thing that I want to mention that helps my creativity is taking a week off after working a few weeks in my clinic and going to an island, a land of sun, sea and sand with my books and papers so that I can finish my unfinished creative projects. All these factors have helped me nurture my creativity. I have developed an affectionate relationship with my muse. She is very kind to me and brings me creative gifts quite frequently. Most artists and writers that I know ignore their creativity. Creativity is a special gift that needs to be taken seriously and nurtured.

AZEEM: Do you see literature as a source of entertainment or a vehicle to share one's philosophy of life?

SOHAIL: Some writers like to entertain and create recreational literature, while others like to enlighten and create serious literature thereby sharing their insights in life. The literature that I respect the most is wisdom literature. Some of the folktales and mystic poetry are part of such wisdom literature.

In my opinion all writers are in search of their truth. After they discover their truth they like to share it with others in a creative way. Those writers who are successful in sharing their profound life experiences and insights in their writings become the representatives of their generation. They offer to humanity new forms of expression and new insights into the human condition.

AZEEM: How are your creative writings different than the writings of your contemporaries?

SOHAIL: Most contemporary writers that I know primarily focus on the form, while my primary focus is on the theme. For me form is secondary. I express myself in many creative forms. I usually pick a theme for my book and then create many poems, essays, stories and translations on that theme. In that way I can collect my observations, experiences, readings and analyses in one book. If you see my books, you will find that the first one is about peace, the second one is about humanism, the third one is about women's liberation and the fourth one is about the struggle of blacks. In my creative writings alongside sharing my truth I also like to raise the social consciousness of my readers, and translating world literature into Urdu is one way of doing that.

**AZEEM**: You are not only a poet and a writer, you are also a psychotherapist. What is your concept of Man?

**SOHAIL**: *As a humanist I have great respect for humanity. I believe that every human child is like a seed that has a unique temperament and potential. For a seed to become a healthy tree and offer wonderful fruits, it needs fertile soil, fresh air, humidity and sunshine. Similarly for a child to become a peace-loving healthy adult he needs love and nurturing and discipline. Children that get all the nurturing they need become successful scientists and artists and politicians and doctors and lawyers, and serve their communities. On the other hand, children who are deprived of love or experience neglect and abuse turn into angry and violent adults. Modern psychology, medicine and literature are helping us find ways to become fully human individually and collectively. I dream of a world where all children will have opportunities to express their full potential.*

**AZEEM**: Over the years you have interviewed many poets and philosophers, writers and artists. What inspires you to do those interviews?

**SOHAIL**: *For me an interview is a creative expression. Socrates taught us that dialogue is one way of discovering truth. Freud noted that interviews can become part of the healing process. To find the right answers in life we need the right questions. The bigger the philosopher, the bigger question he asks. We need to teach our children to ask the right questions to learn and grow. In one hour of interviewing creative personalities I discover the essence of their life* *struggles and the lessons they have learnt in life. A lot of people come to my website to read those interviews.*

**AZEEM**: Many immigrant writers have written about the struggles of living in a foreign land. How do you see the immigrant experience?

**SOHAIL**: *When immigrant writers move from one culture to another they are able to experience two languages, two literatures and two lifestyles in two communities. Experiencing two cultures can open their inner third eye and they can create literature that can become a metaphor of our contemporary world. As far as my personal life is concerned I had more smiles than tears in this journey. By coming to Canada I had many wonderful and inspiring experiences that broadened my existential horizons. My worldview grew and I became a better writer, a better therapist and a better human being. Urdu writers are preoccupied with nostalgia. Many of them are physically living in the West but emotionally living in the East. We are living in a global village and immigrant writers can express the angst of living in this modern mixed community.*

**AZEEM**: Do you consider yourself a socialist?

**SOHAIL**: *I have been inspired by the philosophies of socialism, democracy and humanism. One of the reasons I chose to live in Canada rather than America was its free health care system. When my patients come to see me they do not have to pay me. Our government pays for their care. In America there are millions of citizens who have inadequate health care services and if they do not have health insurance they have great difficulty accessing any health care at all. I think the state should provide housing, education and health care to all citizens. I do not mind paying high taxes to the government so that it can* *provide such services to the needy. I consider that a part of social responsibility. I like to share that responsibility and serve my community as a therapist.*

**AZEEM**: There has been a wave of fundamentalism all over the world and America has been reacting strongly to it. What are your views about this issue?

**SOHAIL**: *When human beings start feeling insecure they regress and become extremists. Fundamentalism is a psychological reaction to world wide anxieties and insecurities. Karen Armstrong in her writings shared the view that in the 20th century there were three waves of fundamentalism. The first one was Christian fundamentalism, the second Jewish fundamentalism and the third Muslim fundamentalism, and each one was more extreme than the previous one. Even the Hindu communities in India are affected by Hindu fundamentalism. When religious fundamentalism became militant it became violent and thousands of innocent men, women and children were killed in the name of God and religion.*

*In my opinion democratic and humanistic values prosper in those communities where:*
*-the gap between different classes is reduced*
*- the literacy rate is raised*
*- people develop social consciousness*
*and*
*- the masses become ready to fight for their human rights.*

*It is very naïve for American politicians to think that by persuading many countries to hold elections they will pave the way for democracy. Democracy is far more complex than elections. Until the social, economic, literacy and human rights issues are resolved, it will be difficult for democracy* to prosper. Even then the democracy implemented in each country has to rise from its own unique traditions. A Western model of democracy may not be acceptable.

**AZEEM**: What are your views about peace?

**SOHAIL**: *In my opinion inner and outer, emotional and social, psychological and political peace are interconnected. It is difficult for people to bring about peace while they are full of anger, resentment and bitterness. I read an article in the Toronto Star in which the writer analyzed people involved in different movements. His analysis was that of all the people involved in political movements only 20% were pro and 80% were against. In the women's movements, more women were taking a stand against men and fewer were working in favour of women. Similarly in the struggle of blacks, the majority were fighting against whites and the minority were campaigning for the rights of blacks. In one interview Mother Teresa had said that she would join a pro-peace rally but not an anti-war rally.*

*I consider war an expression of collective anger and hostility. In my opinion peace is more than absence of war. Peace is a positive, constructive and progressive way of living. During the Cold War there was no war but there was no peace either. Peace comes into existence when both parties are willing to live in harmony and resolve their conflicts respectfully and graciously.*

*I believe world peace is intimately connected with justice. As long as poor countries are exploited by rich countries and there is no justice in the international courts, we will not see lasting peace in the world. I am totally against the veto power of the five countries on the Security Council of the United Nations. All nations of the world need to have power at the United Nations, and the UN should declare our planet a nuclear weapon free zone for global peace. No nation needs to have an army or nuclear weapons. Only the*

United Nations should have a peace force to police the world, and that peace force should consist of soldiers of all the world's nations. How can we have peace in the world when we are living in an era of a war economy and rich nations are thriving by selling weapons to poor countries?

**AZEEM**: How do you see the future of the world?

**SOHAIL**: I believe in human evolution. In my opinion humanity is at a crossroads. We have two choices. We can commit collective suicide through nuclear war, or we can grow to the next stage of human evolution and learn to live peacefully with each other. We need to rise above the tribal mentality in which human beings are at war with other human beings based on different classes, races, languages, religions and nationalities. We need leaders who will promote peace consciousness rather than violent consciousness. We need to find peace
- within ourselves
- with other humans
and
- with nature.

To create a peaceful world together we need to learn that we are all members of the same tribe, the same human family and that our enemies are our distant cousins.

---